PUEBLO POTTERY FAMILIES

ACOMA, COCHITI, HOPI, ISLETA, JEMEZ, LAGUNA, NAMBE, PICURIS, POJOAQUE, SAN ILDEFONSO, SAN JUAN, SANTA CLARA, SANTO DOMINGO, TAOS, TESUQUE, ZIA, ZUNI

LILLIAN PEASTER

Schiffer Publishing Ltd

4880 Lower Valley Road, Atglen, PA 19310

This book is dedicated to my husband
F.M. (Pete) Peaster,
for without his encouragement
this book might never have been written.

Library of Congress Cataloging-in-Publication Data

Peaster, Lillian.
    Pueblo pottery families: Acoma, Cochiti, Hopi, Isleta, Jemez, Laguna,
Nambe, Picuris, Pojoaque, San Ildefonso, San Juan, Santa Clara, Santo
Domingo, Taos, Tesuque, Zia, Zuni/Lillian Peaster.
    p. cm.
    Includes index.
    ISBN 0-7643-0233-7
    1. Pueblo pottery--Collectors and collecting. 2. Pueblo pottery--
Directories. I. Title.
E99.P9P35 1997
738.3'089'974--dc21   97-3643
                                                      CIP

All photographs by the author unless otherwise noted.

Designed by "Sue"
ISBN: 0-7643-0233-7
Printed in China

Front Cover
Contemporary pueblo pottery.
Top left: B.J. Fragua, Jemez
Right: Dextra Quotskuyva, Hopi
Center: pot with turquoise, Dora Tse Pe, San Ildefonso
Bottom right: Denise Chavarria, Santa Clara
Bottom left: Frances Torvino, Acoma.
Courtesy of Mark Bahtis Shop. Photo by Paul Berquist, Ray Manley Studio

Published by Schiffer Publishing Ltd.
4880 Lower Valley Road
Atglen, PA 19310
Phone: (610) 593-1777; Fax: (610) 593-2002
E-mail: schifferbk@aol.com
Please write for a free catalog.
This book may be purchased from the publisher.
Please include $2.95 for shipping.
Try your bookstore first.

We are interested in hearing from authors
with book ideas on related subjects.

Contents

ACKNOWLEDGEMENTS

My thanks are extended to:

Brenda Cosse for typing the family trees,

Nadia Caillou for typing the manuscript,

Toni Roller for allowing me to live at her place when I was researching Santa Clara potters,

Joseph and Kathy Lonewolf for taking time out from a busy schedule for almost two days to visit,

Rosemary Lonewolf who moved to New Jersey, heard from her brother Gregory about the book, and sent many pages of information and a photo of herself and her son Adam,

Marie Romero of Jemez for her hospitality and encouragement,

my husband Pete who drove thousands of miles without complaining and ate too many hot New Mexico meals and did complain,

and last, but not least, my great appreciation goes to all the potters in this book. I love them all and cherish my many friendships with them.

PREFACE

Southwest American Indian pottery is an art form not only alive and well today but actually booming business in some pueblos and the prices keep climbing. Some potters tell me that they give themselves a small raise each year.

I have always admired Indian pottery and have been a collector of it for years, but it was while I was working part-time at Ninebah's, an Indian shop in my hometown of Sedona, Arizona, that I realized the need for this book. Pottery customers were always inquiring about who the potters were and where they lived. Collectors would ask about members of certain families. They had perhaps three pieces of pottery made by members of one family and wanted to "complete that family."

Since the names Tafoya, Naranjo and Gutierrez are as common as Smith and Jones in the Anglo world, their same last names do not always mean that the potters are related. There are several Lewis families living at Acoma who are not related to Lucy Lewis. There are Chinos who are not related to the Marie Chino Family. We need help sorting them out.

This book presents the work and the family trees of many of the current Pueblo potters. Each family tree has been given and verified by at least two family members. I met many wonderful and talented people while traveling through the Pueblos who were cooperative, friendly, and helpful. They all wanted to make sure their information was correct, and most asked to see their family trees after they were completed. Some potters would have been included if I had been made aware of them. A few modestly declined to be photographed. Others were not available for interviews, and I felt that it was absolutely necessary to personally interview family members before writing about them. I would like to stress to the readers that potters who are not listed here are no less talented or accomplished than those who are. Because the focus of this book is the potters, non-potters and young children may have been left off the family trees. Some non-potters have been included when I was given their information by the family. I hope readers will find this book helpful in learning more about the people who make this beautiful pottery. Its writing has not been a simple task, but a grueling, yet enjoyable one.

I learned much by talking with other collectors, and especially from the "traders," the men and women who bring the pottery to us from the pueblos. The Hopi prefer to bring their wares to us themselves; they don't care to deal with the middle man, but a lot of them have to.

Visiting with the potters was a great joy for me, and some of them have become dear friends. We visit each other; we share the joys and sorrows and worries of life. I have watched all phases of pottery-making and the firing. To me, the sanding is the worse part — very dusty — so many of the potters wear masks when doing this work. My very best wishes go out to all the Native American potters who still make pottery the old way and fire their pots outside with manure as fuel. However, I would encourage the collector not to become entangled with the word "tradition." I have not gone into great details to explain the making and firing of the pottery, for there are numerous excellent books on the market explaining these steps. My interest is in correctly identifying the pottery with its makers. Entire books have been written about the work of only one potter, such as Maria Martinez, Margaret Tafoya and Lucy Lewis. Don't expect to purchase their pots at a cheap price--if you can find them. There is a wide variety of Native American pottery in galleries, shops, and museums now. Not all of it is good, but it is found in every price range from a few dollars up to the thousands. (See the Values Reference at the end of the book.) Buy what appeals to you, not for investment but as something you can look at every day and enjoy.

The art of pottery-making is currently thriving in most of the pueblos today. Small amounts of pottery are also made at Santa Ana, Sandia, and San Felipe Pueblos.

Many times there are three generations still working together; the younger ones taking advice from the older ones until they develop their own designs. They each wait to be introduced to you on the following pages.

ACOMA PUEBLO

Acoma Pueblo is famous for its beautiful white, thin-walled pottery with bright-orange parrots, rainbows, and Mimbres figures of people, lizards, and ladybugs painted on them. Each potter has his or her secret source of clay. They grind old pottery shards and put it in the clay as a temper or binder.

Acoma, also known as Sky City, is a famous landmark - a huge rock formation - with a beautiful old chapel built in the 1600s. There are approximately twelve or thirteen families who live there year round. Their only source of water is rainwater caught in the cisterns. There is no soil except what the Indians take up from below and there is no electricity. Sky City elevation is 6,400 feet above sea level.

Below, in the villages of Acomita, McCartys, and San Fidel, there are some 4,000 people living. Many of them make pottery in the old traditional way. A number of others use greenware, or commercial pottery. It is hand-painted and is priced much cheaper than the traditionally made pottery. Some today fire their pots in an electric kiln instead of over a wood fire. See photographs of the wood firing procedure by Gladys Paquin in the Laguna Pueblo chapter.

Storyteller by Peggy Garcia, Acoma

Santa Maria Chapel at McCartys

LUCY M. LEWIS (-1992)

Lucy Lewis was the matriarch of Acoma pottery. She began making pots as a small child and sold it along old Highway 66. Over the years her skills steadily grew, but she didn't start signing her work until around 1963. Although her birth was never recorded, her family believed her to be in her mid-nineties when she died on March 12, 1992. When I visited Lucy, it was difficult to communicate with her, as she was quite hard of hearing. Shortly after that visit she fell and her health declined steadily. Her daughters gave me the true family tree and asked me to let people know that only those listed on the family chart are members of the family.

Lucy had won many awards for her work, including the Governor's Award for Excellence and Achievement, which is New Mexico's highest award. Her work is on display in museums and galleries around the world.

Lucy's greatest legacy is her family of five daughters, two sons, three granddaughters, and one great-granddaughter, all of whom are fine potters. Daughters Mary Garcia and Ann Hanson live in California but visited their mother often. Dolores Garcia, Emma Mitchell, and Carmela Haskaya showed me the proce-

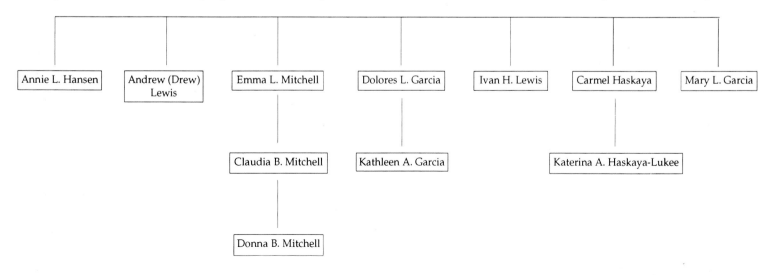

dures they go through to make their pottery. Delores said that the public expects a perfect pot, with no fire clouds that arise from windy conditions on the reservation. To meet this requirement, a large percentage of Acoma pottery is fired in kilns. Acoma handmade pots are very thin-walled and have a "bell sound" when thumped on the top.

Lucy Lewis family, left to right:
Front: Emma L. Mitchell, Lucy M. Lewis, Dolores L. Garcia
Back: Katherine Lukee, Carmel Lewis, Donna Mitchell
Photo by Murrae Haynes

Top: Bowl by Lucy Lewis
Left: Vase by Carmel Lewis
Center: Small vase by Donna Mitchell
Right: Bowl by Emma Lewis Mitchell

FRANCES TORIVIO (1905-)

Frances Torivio was born on April 1, 1905, at Sky City, the old Acoma Pueblo. She learned to make her thin-walled pots in the traditional coil-and-scrape method by watching and helping her mother. She paints her pottery with a yucca brush, using only natural earth and mineral colors. Her style is traditional, using the four traditional geometrical designs representing the four directions and seasons. Sometimes she includes flowers, a rainbow -- which represents good luck -- and animals, such as the parrot, the favorite bird of Acoma.

Her work has won numerous awards at the Santa Fe Indian Markets. She even has a prize piece, delivered by her grandson and exhibited at the Soviet National Museum.

Besides making pots, Frances organized (in 1976) and taught classes in order to help revive pottery-making among her people. She is now semi-retired, making a few small pots and storytellers and assisting her daughters in their pottery making. Most of all, it seems, she enjoys being with her grandchildren and great-grandchildren.

Left to right: Frances Torvino and daughters Maria Lily Salvador and Wanda Aragon

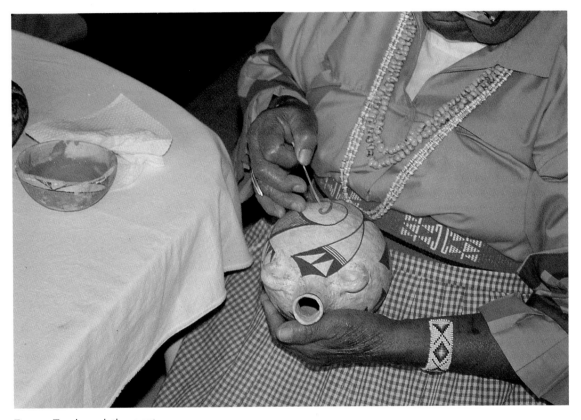

Frances Torvino painting a pot

LILLY SALVADOR

Lilly's artistic abilities include pottery, weaving, painting, silversmithing, and native embroidery. She is best known for the beautiful, thin-walled pottery for which she has received many awards. She was taught by her mother, noted Acoma potter Frances Torivio, using native clay mixed with finely ground pot shards. Her paints are ground sandstone, mixed with vegetable dyes, all found on the Acoma Reservation. Her husband Wayne digs and prepares clay for the family.

On her four directional pottery designs, Lilly purposely leaves the linebreak at the bottom of the pot, so as not to imprison the spirits brought forth from the pot.

Lilly has a gallery at the foot of Sky City where, along with her own work, she sells the pottery of her family. Her daughters Carleen and Darlene have both won awards. Another daughter, Roberta, paints greenware, and Lilly's son Ryan Paul is beginning to work with the clay.

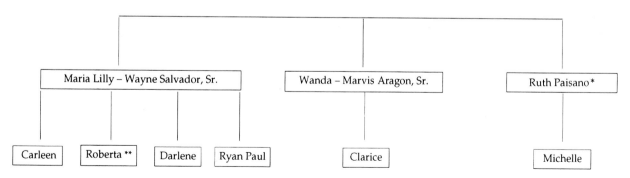

Frances Torivio

| Maria Lilly – Wayne Salvador, Sr. | Wanda – Marvis Aragon, Sr. | Ruth Paisano* |

Carleen | Roberta ** | Darlene | Ryan Paul | Clarice | Michelle

**Roberta paints greenware.

*Deceased

Migration pot by Lilly Salvador and small canteen by Wanda Aragon

GIVE LIFE AND BEAUTY

With gentle hands and feet,
I mix my native clay,
tempered with old pot shards ground to powder-like substance.

With gentle hands, coil by coil
I create these pots and figurines.

With precision strokes of my yucca-fiber brush I outline the design;
Native colored clay and sandstone paints beautify and enhance my creations.

Into the mound of sheep and cow dung, my creations go...
I pray to the almighty spirits -- Give life and beauty....

LILLY (Acoma Potter)
Written by Lilly and Wayne Salvador

Migration vase by
Maria Lilly Salvador

Lilly's sister Wanda Aragon is a fine potter and has won many awards. Wanda's daughter Clarice is following in her mother's footsteps.

Wanda Aragon, pottery & family

JOSEPH AND BARBARA CERNO

Joseph and Barbara Cerno make the largest pots I have ever seen. They also make tiny seed pots as well as regular sizes.

The Eight Northern Indian Pueblos Artist and Craftsman Show was held at the San Juan Pueblo in 1991. For a huge pot, they received three ribbons: Best of Show, Best of Category, and Best All Around. This pot took Joseph many months to make. He makes the big pots and creates the designs; Barbara does the painting. Joseph goes to museums to study old Acoma designs, so he will be sure of their accuracy.

Their son, Joseph Jr., also a potter, has won several awards.

Barbara and Joseph sign all their work "B & J Cerno". Sometimes, in bad weather, they fire in a kiln; however, the large pots must be fired outside because they won't fit into a kiln.

Barbara and Joseph Cerno, prize winners at the Eight Northern Show,

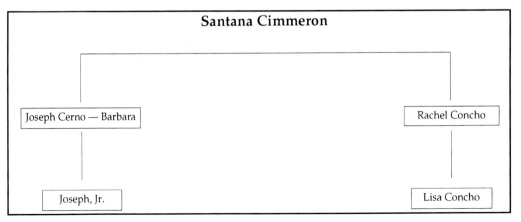

Barbara and Joseph Cerno's prize winner

Santana Cimmeron, Joseph's mother, is a potter. At the age of almost one hundred, she gets around with the aid of a walker. She enjoys having visitors and discussing the old methods.

Rachel Concho, sister to Joseph, makes small, delicate seed pots. She has been an exhibitor at the Eight Northern Indian Pueblos Arts and Crafts Show since its beginning 21 years ago. She has received numerous awards at Eight Northern, including Best of Show. She has participated in Indian Market in Santa Fe. In 1992 she was commissioned by the Coca Cola Company to make 450 pieces for them. That commission was renewed in 1993.

Santana Cimmeron

THE CHINO FAMILY

Another well-known pottery family is the Chinos. Offspring of the late Marie Z. Chino, they are daughters Rose Garcia, Grace Chino (who died in 1994), Carrie Charlie, son Patrick, and adopted daughter Jody. All are potters as are several grand-, and great-grandchildren. Most of them make pottery atop Sky City, and it is available for sale there as well as in some galleries.

The Chino Family: Carrie C. Charlie, Rose C. Garcia, Grace Chino. Photo by Murrae Haynes

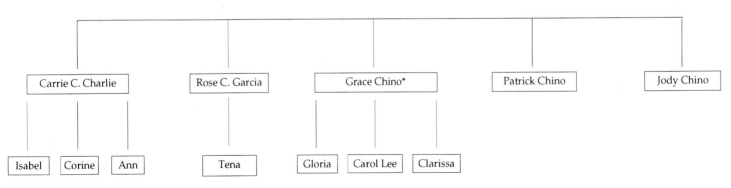

*Deceased

Carrie Charlie, Rose Garcia, and Grace Chino and their pots

Jackie Shutiva Histia

Jackie, the second daughter of the late Stella Shutiva, is one of six children and the only one making pottery and thereby carrying on her mother's belief that traditional Acoma pottery must be kept alive.

Stella was famous for her large corrugated pots. It took Jackie almost four years to learn this method. In the old days, potters pinched each coil with their fingers. Today's potters leave the coils untouched on the outside, then texture all at one time with a pointed tool.

When her mother passed away, Jackie's father gave her the tools her mother had used, which included an octagon-shaped carpenter's pencil used to corrugate the coils.

Jackie has persuaded her husband, Bennett Histia, to join her in full time pottery-making, using designs and symbols that relate to their Pueblo culture.

Due to the demand for their pottery and the attention required to care for their baby, they hire men to dig clay for them. Because their pots are so white, rumors in the Pueblo have suggested they use commercial clay. Not true: Jackie showed me their clay in different stages of preparation.

They do fire in a kiln to keep the pots white, to prevent fire clouds, and to protect the delicate appliques of corn and other decorations. This information was given to me by Jackie.

Jackie and Greg Histia

Corrugated wedding vase by Jackie Shutiva Histia

ETHEL SHIELDS

Ethel was taught to make pottery by her mother, Dolores Sanchez (now deceased), approximately fifty years ago. At the age of twelve, she began making small pieces and learning to polish. Today, Ethel is a skilled potter. She makes traditional as well as contemporary Acoma pottery.

Several years ago, she and a cousin took a trip to Mesa Verde Museum, just outside Cortez, Colorado. Ethel was fascinated by the shapes of the old canteens and pitchers. They took many photographs of them. After returning home, she studied the photos carefully. She began to make canteens in the shapes of turtles, ears of corn, snakes, and other animals; also pitchers with faces, arms, and hands. In both arms she placed one or more babies. She painted them all with the same Anasazi colors and designs she had seen at the museum.

Of Ethel's several children, she has taught pottery-making to one daughter, Charmae, and two daughters-in-law, Judy and Verda Mae Shields. She also helped her son-in-law Thomas Natseway.

Judy Shields makes exquisite miniature storytellers. Verda Mae Shields makes beautiful Christmas ornaments.

Unfinished pots by Ethel Shields

Left to right: Thomas Natseway, Charmae Shields Natseway, Judy Shields, Ethel Shields

THOMAS NATSEWAY AND CHARMAE SHIELDS NATSEWAY

Thomas is a member of the Laguna tribe. He had chosen journalism as a career until 1979 when he was working for a newspaper and conducting interviews with Acoma artists. There he met Charmae Shields. He was impressed with the three generations of pottery on display at her mother's home. He and Charmae were soon married. They lived with her mother, Ethel Shields. His wife and mother-in-law taught Thomas to make pottery. Not wanting to compete with them, he chose to make miniatures. His are smaller than a thimble with designs ranging from flowers and butterflies to the Acoma fine geometric lines, and the Zuni interlocking swirls.

At the present time, he doesn't use magnification devices. A piece of clay the size of a finger will make eighteen or more pots.

Thomas sometimes helps Charmae with the painting of her pots. She makes lovely seed pots in all sizes and all with the old Acoma designs. Especially beautiful are the old Mimbres designs with lizards and bugs. Charmae's unusually shaped pots include boxes, pyramids, and cylinders.

The family has a wall full of ribbons they have won at shows, especially at Indian Markets.

Right: Kayenta miniature water jug by Thomas Natseway
Left: Owl Storyteller by Judy Shields
Photo by Peter Bloomer

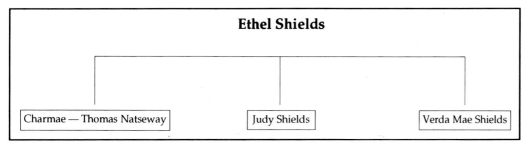

Ethel Shields

Charmae — Thomas Natseway | Judy Shields | Verda Mae Shields

Judy and Verda Mae are daughters-in-law.

COCHITI PUEBLO

Cochiti is an enterprising pueblo. They have built, away from their village but on Cochiti land, a golf course with pro-shop and snack bar and beautiful, modern homes that are rented to non-Indians for retirement homes. They also have a large lake which is a popular picnic place.

The road out of Cochiti leads to Santo Domingo, without the need to return to Interstate 25.

Cochiti pottery, clockwise from left: figure with drum by Seferina Ortiz; canteen by Laurencita Herrera; singing figure by Virgil Ortiz; appliqued bowl by Ivan Lewis
Photo by Murrae Haynes

HELEN CORDERO (-1994)

Helen Cordero claims to be the originator of clay storytellers. There is some controversy within the pueblo that others were making them before Helen; however, no proof has been shown.

Helen modeled her first storyteller after her great-grandfather who was a storyteller himself. He would tell stories to all his family as the grandchildren would gather around, climb all over him, and sit on his lap. This is how Helen got the idea for the clay storytellers.

When she lost sight in one eye and had poor vision in the other, her doctor had advised her not to work with the clay any more, but she continued; she had been doing it so long that making storytellers was in her blood.

Her daughter Toni Suina assisted her with the sanding and firing.

ELIZABETH "BUFFY" CORDERO SUINA

Buffy, as she is called, was taught the art of making Storytellers by her grandmother, Helen Cordero. Buffy has been making pottery for twelve years.

She also makes other figures such as drummers, Navajo women Storytellers and turtles. The turtles have a story behind them. They were heroic animals in a story Helen Cordero's great-grandfather used to tell:

It happened that there was a great war among all the tribes. The giant turtles came to the aid of the children. They carried the children on their backs to safety until the war was ended, and the parents could care for them again.

Buffy is a personable young lady who takes great pride in making her pottery the traditional way. She signs each piece, "Buffy Cordero-Suina, Cochiti Pueblo."

Buffy Cordero Suina and her storyteller

Mary Frances Herrera (-1991)

Mary Frances Herrera made small, happy-looking storytellers with arms full of happy children. Her daughters Dorothy and Mary Ramona make the same size and style as their late mother did. A son, Edwin, makes bear storytellers. His wife, also named Mary, paints them black and Edwin finishes them. Dorothy also makes bears.

Mary Ramona is called Mona by her family because there are two Marys in the same house. She signs her pieces "M.H." I asked if she could sign M. Herrera so people would know that she is Mary Frances' daughter. Their work is so alike that I can't tell them apart. They all use commercial paints.

Edwin and Mary Herrera and their new baby

Dorothy Herrera and sons

SEFERINA ORTIZ

Seferina Ortiz and her husband Guadalupe are pleasant to visit with and eager to explain every step in making her wonderful storytellers. She is the potter and he is a drum-maker. She wants to teach him pottery-making so he can help her. She always has orders to fill and her storytellers are much in demand.

Many, many coats of white slip must be applied over the red clay they use. Most of the Cochiti potters used to buy the slip from Santo Domingo, but the prices have gone up, so Seferina and Guadalupe are searching for slip clay on Cochiti land. After getting permission from a friend to dig on his property, Guadalupe dug down twelve feet before he located

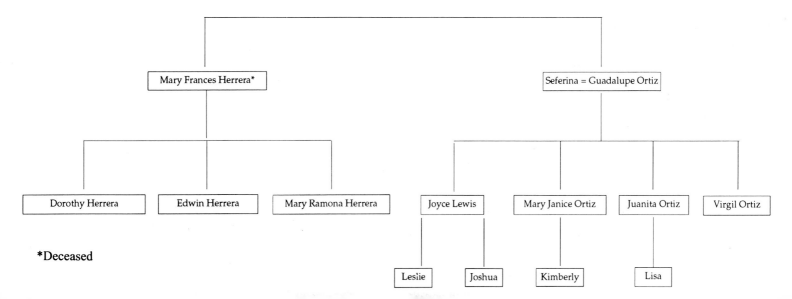

Laurincita* – Nestor Herrera*

Mary Frances Herrera*
- Dorothy Herrera
- Edwin Herrera
- Mary Ramona Herrera

Seferina = Guadalupe Ortiz
- Joyce Lewis
  - Leslie
  - Joshua
- Mary Janice Ortiz
  - Kimberly
- Juanita Ortiz
  - Lisa
- Virgil Ortiz

*Deceased

Seferina Ortiz puts finishing touches on her bear storyteller

a small quantity of usable slip. If their pottery seems expensive, remember it is the result of very hard work.

Seferina learned to make pottery from her mother, Laurencita Herrera, in the 1960s. Laurencita was also mother of the late Mary Frances Herrera. Seferina has won numerous prizes for her work, and some of her pieces are on permanent display in museums. In addition to human storytellers, she does frog, turtle, and owl storytellers, and mermaids, bowls and jars.

LOUIS AND VIRGINIA NARANJO

Louis and Virginia Naranjo both grew up in Cochiti, married, and had a family. Virginia would help Louis's mother, Frances Suina, with the firing of her pottery and was encouraged by Frances to start making small pieces. At that time, Virginia was working at the Cochiti school and Louis worked off-pueblo. Virginia became an accomplished potter making storytellers and winning awards for her work. After she had a stroke, fell, and broke her arm, she began to teach Louis to make figurines. Once, when he was out hunting, he saw a mother bear with her cubs crawling all over her. It was then that he decided to make bear storytellers. He was the first in Cochiti to make them; now there are many others who make bear storytellers.

It took a lot of encouragement from Virginia to keep Louis making pottery. After he retired from his full time job, he had more free time, so he really got into making figurines. In addition to bears, he makes nativity scenes as well as Santa Claus, priest, and fox storytellers. He also makes Cochiti dancing figurines. Virginia doesn't make pottery anymore, but she does most of the sanding with the help of their daughter, Pauline Naranjo.

Louis Naranjo working on a bear storyteller

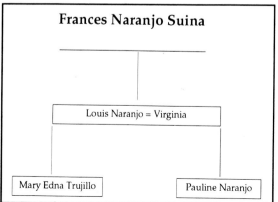

Frances Naranjo Suina

Louis Naranjo = Virginia

Mary Edna Trujillo	Pauline Naranjo

IVAN LEWIS

Ivan comes from a long line of potters. He is the son of the late, great potter Lucy Lewis from Acoma Pueblo. He left Acoma to marry Rita Banada at Cochiti Pueblo. Rita was taught by her mother.

Ivan always helped Rita with the pottery, but only after he retired did Rita convince him to start making his own pieces. Rita passed away in 1991. Ivan makes storytellers, dough bowls, and whimsical figurines. He is unable to fire his pottery outside in the traditional way because of his health, so he fires in a kiln.

Ivan's daughter Patricia is a teacher at Cochiti, but makes pottery in her spare time. Her young daughter, Vanessa, born in 1986, is learning. Patricia's son, Kevin, has already won many awards for his work.

Ivan's son Ronald and his wife Tomasita work together making pottery. Another of Ivan's sons, Elmer, does not pot, but his wife Mary is a potter.

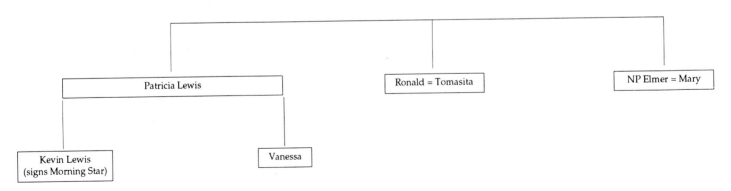

Ivan Lewis = Rita Banada*

- Patricia Lewis
  - Kevin Lewis (signs Morning Star)
  - Vanessa
- Ronald = Tomasita
- NP Elmer = Mary

*Deceased

Ivan Lewis with a bowl and a storyteller

HOPI PUEBLO

THE MYSTIC HOPI MESAS

The Hopi Indians have lived for centuries on three mesas in northern Arizona. First Mesa is where most of the potters live, in the villages of Polacca, Hano, Walpi and Sichomovi. The potters also extend to Keams Canyon and a little beyond.

First Mesa is known for its beautiful pottery. Second Mesa is known for the coiled baskets and plaques made there. Third Mesa is where the tribal offices are located in the village of Kykotsmovi. In each of the three mesas live silversmiths, kachina doll carvers, and makers of wicker baskets.

Hopi pottery is changing. The old designs are still being used, and always will be, but more contemporary pieces also are showing up for sale at trading posts and galleries. Hopi pottery has become more innovative than pottery at most of the other pueblos.

The electric kiln has found its way to Hopi, and some think pots fired in a kiln look dead; that there is no spirit, no joy, no life and it shows. Kiln use, however, is not wide-spread; recently only a few kiln fired pieces have been seen in shops. Potters today use a kiln when unable to fire outside.

Pottery, clockwise from left:
Jar by Claudina Lomakema;
shallow bowl by Helen Naha;
Jar by Jean Nampeyo; bowl by
Marsha Rickey
Center: Tall jar by Joy Navasie
Center front: bowl by Sadie
Adams
Photo by Murrae Haynes

HELEN NAHA (FEATHER WOMAN) (-1992)

There are two families at Hopi who specialize in making white pottery; the Nahas are one of them. They use pure white clay, and create their own unique designs. Helen taught her three children to make pottery when they were very young. It was part of their chores after school to help with sanding or gathering the clay. She taught them to reach into the pot as far as they could reach to polish the inside, sometimes they had to use their fingernails to make it smooth in small places.

Helen signed her work with a large, brown, plumed feather. Her children do the same on their pots and add their first initial so people will know which Naha made the pot. Helen and her husband had a cattle ranch about fifteen miles from Polacca. The family is kept busy taking care of the ranch, their families, and the demand for their pottery. They work together in harmony and get the job done. Helen was a potter for over fifty years.

Pottery by Helen Naha

Pottery by Sylvia Naha

SYLVIA NAHA

Sylvia and her family are multi-talented. They all make unique Hopi pottery, using white clay from a nearby mesa. After shaping the pot, many coats of slip are applied and the last coat is polished; then it is ready to be decorated. Sylvia uses a wooden kitchen match to help smooth the coils and for the stippling. The family uses the same designs with their own details incorporated. When Sylvia was a little girl, her father found a pot while working in his cornfield. The designs on this pot became the Naha family trademark. Sylvia makes only small to medium pots. Her design includes the cross-hatch, similar to some designs at Acoma. She uses a tiny yucca brush for detailing and painting. There is an unwritten code of ethics that when a potter takes on a design for his or her family, no one else copies it. Sylvia signs her pots with a large, brown, plumed feather, and the initial S.

Sylvia Naha (in the blue blouse) and her cousin, Cynthia Sequi Komalestewa, also a potter

Pottery, clockwise from left: Black on white by Sylvia Naha;
bowl by Marsha Rickey; jar by Nampeyo; seed bowl by
Stella Huma; jar by Nathan Begay
Photo by Murrae Haynes

BUREL NAHA

Burel Naha has made some traditions of his own. Part of his chores as a child, along with his sisters, was to help make pottery. He sanded and helped to gather the pure white clay.

After high school, he attended Brigham Young University in Utah where he received a degree in art. He taught art at the University, then moved to Blandings, Utah, to teach art. Four years later, he moved to Phoenix, Arizona, and worked for the Phoenix Indian School in the administrative offices. After this job, he returned home to the Hopi mesas where he built a beautiful home for his large family.

During these years, he continued to develop his own artistic talents. His acrylic paintings on canvas of the kachinas are quite beautiful and he carves kachina dolls.

He began making pottery about five years ago using the family designs, but he wanted a design all his own. One day his daughter, Cynthia, brought home from school a sticker with a large black spider on it. It caught Burel's eye and he thought about it a lot. He began with tiny brushes, painting large eight-legged spiders, their bellies full of designs. Burel says that spiders are not a part of Hopi designs but he has made them his tradition. He makes a good living with his art and is teaching his children; his son Michael is already a good carver. Burel's Indian name is "Long Hair Kachina Feather". He signs his beautiful pottery with a plumed feather and a "B", and also draws on the Long Hair Kachina Feather design.

Spider vase by Burel Naha

Burel Naha and his sister Raynelle

Raynelle Naha

Raynelle, or Rainey as she is called, has been making pottery for about seven years. She is not as prolific as the rest of the family, only makeing a few little pots a month.

She lives next door to her brother, Burel, and I sensed a great closeness between the two of them. Rainey uses a popsicle stick to smooth the coils, then licks - yes, licks - them completely smooth. She knows before she shapes a pot which designs she will use, and shapes the pot accordingly.

Rainey attended Brigham Young University in Utah, studied archeology, but did not graduate. She moved to Blandings, Utah, and lived there for a while. She has been back home at Hopi for about eleven years keeping very busy doing volunteer work as needed. She is a runner, and competes in races for the benefit of drug and alcohol-rehabilitation centers.

Rainey has a very upbeat personality and is full of energy; she helps with the cattle at her parents' ranch. Her work is signed with the feathered plume and the initial R.

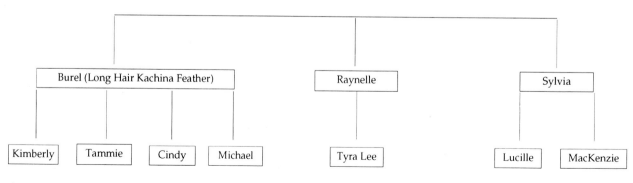

Helen Naha (Feather Woman)*

*Deceased

VERLA DEWAKUKU

Verla's family doesn't have a large number of potters; only her daughter Iva Namingha, and Iva's daughter Denise have taken to the clay. Verla lives in Hano, next to Walpi, on the first mesa. During the summer season, she is kept busy making small pots that sell for a reasonable price. Verla's husband is a kachina carver, so between them they make a living.

Verla uses the red clay and her designs are her own creations. One that I like is the stylized butterfly. Iva makes buff colored pots using old Hopi designs. Denise makes little clay animals. Verla fires both traditionally and in a kiln.

KAREN CHARLEY

Karen learned from her mother, Marcella Kahe, and has been potting for about eight years. She won Best of Division for a canteen at Santa Fe Indian Market. She has been attending the Indian Market and other shows for ten years and always wins ribbons. She won first place at the Northern Arizona Museum Show in Flagstaff, Arizona, two years in a row.

GLORIA KAHE

Gloria is a Navajo lady who grew up with her sheep herding family on the Navajo Reservation. She married Karen Charley's brother, Sam Kahe. Gloria learned to make pottery by watching and helping her mother-in-law, Marcella Kahe. Marcella was awarded the Living Treasure Award as a potter in 1993.

Gloria learned fast, and soon her beautiful pottery was in much demand. A few of her awards include a first place medal from Red Earth, Oklahoma City, Oklahoma, and numerous ribbons for best of classification and others first, second, and third places.

Her husband, Sam, is also an artist, a kachina carver, and painter of gourds with Hopi pottery designs. He prepares the clay for Gloria and helps with the firing.

Gloria has an adult daughter, Valerie, who recently has become a potter. She and Gloria both use Hopi designs on their pottery.

Karen Charley, left, with two small, unfired plaques and Gloria Kahe with an unfired vase

JOY NAVASIE (FROG WOMAN) AND FAMILY

Joy has been a potter for many years, and comes from a family of potters. She uses the white clay, the same as the Naha family; Joy is the sister of Helen Naha's husband.

Joy and her husband, Perry, have a large family that now makes the pots and Joy paints the designs. They all use the frog as a hallmark, so when you see the frog you have only part of the clue about who made the piece. Joy's daughter, Grace, signs her work with a frog, and somewhere in the design she incorporates a tadpole. Her three sons sign their work the same way.

Joy's son, Maynard, and his wife, Veronica, sign with their initials "M.N. & V.N." along with the frog. Their son Bill, whose work is outstanding, signs with a frog surrounded by large musical notes. His Hopi name is "Tu tuk ya" which means "frog that sings after the rains". Bill's brother, Raynard Navasie, seldom makes pottery.

Loretta Kashway is another of Joy's daughters and they work together. Joy does all the painting. Loretta's son, Charles Navasie, also signs with a frog. Another of Joy's daughters, Leona Navasie, lives in Tuba City, approximately seventy

Joy Navasie = Perry Navasie NP

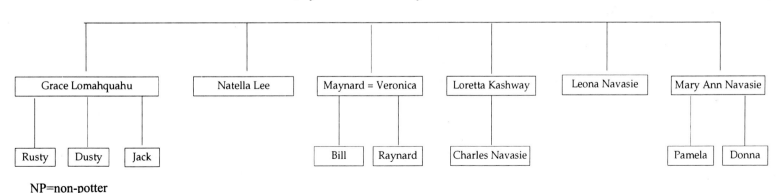

NP=non-potter

Pot by Maynard and Veronica Navasie

five miles from Joy, and only makes pottery during the summer months. Joy paints Leona's pots.

Yet another daughter of Joy is Mary Ann Navasie who designs and paints the pots made by her daughters, Pamela and Donna. Mary Ann is left-handed, and her swirls and designs drift to the left. Pamela signs her pots "P.N." with a frog on the bottom and a tadpole in the design. Donna does the same with her initials, D.N.

Still another of Joy's daughters is Netella Lee who knows the basics, but rarely makes pottery.

This information was given to me by Grace when I stopped to see Joy and her family. I asked Joy if I could take her picture, but she declined; she said she hated to have her picture taken. I respect her decision.

DAWN NAVASIE

Dawn is the second daughter of the late Fawn Navasie. Fawn, a sister to Joy Navasie's husband, Perry, was killed in 1992 by a hit-and-run driver in Holbrook, Arizona.

Fawn was an outstanding potter, and she taught her three daughters well. Dawn is very meticulous with the polishing and the painting. Everything is traditional and she fires outside in her back yard.

Dawn's sister Dolly Joe is married to a Navajo man and they live with Dawn. Dolly's work is also outstanding and she signs her work "White Swan". Their other sister is Little Fawn who is married to James Garcia, a potter from the Nampeyo family. They live in Kykotsmovi on Third Mesa.

Fawn Navasie *

| Little Fawn = James Garcia Nampeyo | Dawn Navasie | Dolly Joe |

*Deceased

DIANNA TAHBO

Dianna Tahbo has only been making pottery since 1989, but to look at her work one would think she has been a potter for much longer. Her designs are the old Hopi patterns, bold and flowing.

She uses sheep manure for firing, because it fires so hot. It also has a very strong odor. Just follow your nose on Polacca and you will find the potters. Once removed from the ashes and cleaned, her pots are a deep golden color with black designs.

Dianna and her brother Mark often fire their pots together. Mark makes some very large pots. He gathers the clay from First Mesa, goes to his apartment in Flagstaff, Arizona, to make the pottery, and returns to Polacca to fire it. Dianna and Mark both have won many awards at Indian Markets as well as at other shows.

Dianna and Mark Tahbo are the great-grandchildren of the late Grace Chappela who made pottery until she died at the age of one hundred and six.

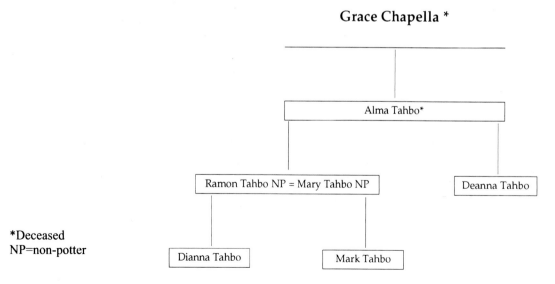

Grace Chapella *

Alma Tahbo*

Ramon Tahbo NP = Mary Tahbo NP

Deanna Tahbo

Dianna Tahbo

Mark Tahbo

*Deceased
NP=non-potter

Dianna Tahbo

Pot by Dianna Tahbo

Nampeyo

Nampeyo was the only name this lady had until she married John Lesso. As you will see by the family tree, they had four children. They are all deceased now, but left behind many grandchildren, who learned pottery-making from their parents and Nampeyo.

Nampeyo saw shards and pots from the old village of Sikyatki. She liked the designs, added some of her own, and the rest is history. It is easy to spot a Nampeyo pot, once you become familiar with the design. Most, but not all, of the third and fourth generations make the Nampeyo designs on their pottery, some of which is very contemporary looking. Most of the potters sign "Nampeyo" at the end of their names.

I was able to locate and visit some of the very busy people in the Nampeyo families. Winter was a bad time to see them because they are preparing for the Kachina dances, only open to Indians. Summer wasn't good either, because there are the social dances, but white people may attend these. So I took my chances, and found a few each trip.

It should be noted that Nampeyo never signed a pot. She could neither read nor write.

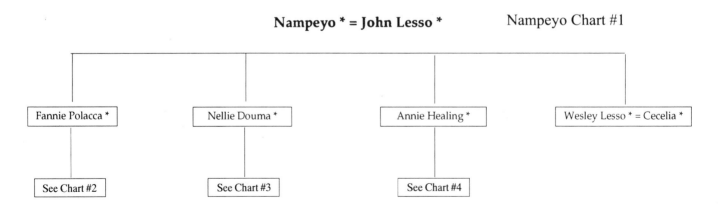

Nampeyo * = John Lesso *   Nampeyo Chart #1

| Fannie Polacca * | Nellie Douma * | Annie Healing * | Wesley Lesso * = Cecelia * |

| See Chart #2 | See Chart #3 | See Chart #4 | |

*Deceased

JAMES GARCIA

James is a traditional potter in every sense of the word. When I visited him, he was painting Nampeyo designs on a pot. He uses a tiny yucca brush about an inch long and very thin. He draws the designs on the pot lightly with a pencil; then, with his hand ever so steady, he dips the brush into the earth paint and applies it to the pot: eagle wing tips, swirls and loops appear and very soon, the pot comes alive.

Traditional Nampeyo pot by James G. Nampeyo

Pots by James G. Nampeyo ready to fire

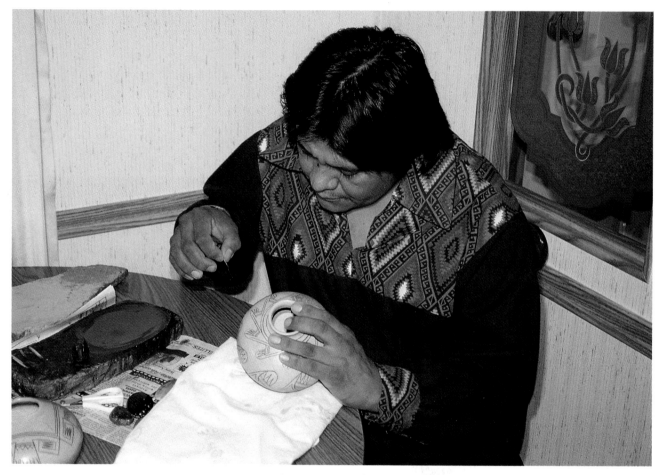

James G. Nampeyo painting a pot

Jar ready for firing by James G. Nampeyo

THOMAS POLACCA

Thomas is the son of the late Fannie Nampeyo Polacca. Thomas's pottery is very different: three-layered and carved. The tops are enclosed with open sides, and carved showing a pueblo village, and a kiva with a ladder going down into it. His pieces are complex and beautiful. Thomas signs his work "Thomas Polacca" or "Thomas P. Nampeyo".

Thomas has three children, Gary, Carla, and Elvira, who are all potters. Carla makes her own designs rather than using Sikyatki designs. Most of her pieces are small, incised with a butterfly design and other insects and animals. They are very highly polished brown. She lives in Tuba City and signs her pots "C.R. Claw Nampeyo." Elvira lives with her father.

James learned to pot from his late mother, Leah Garcia. After she died, he went to live with his grandmother, Fannie Nampeyo Polacca. Under her guidance, he became a perfectionist. For the past twelve years he has made his living at pottery-making. He married Little Fawn Navasie, daughter of the late Fawn Navasie. They work together on their pottery. She signs her work "Little Fawn" with a tiny hoof-print. James signs his work "James G. Nampeyo."

IRIS YOUVELLA

Iris is a sister to Thomas Polacca whose specialty is pots of all sizes with corn appliques on the sides. She makes some others, but the "corn pots" are the best sellers; they are always in demand. Her pots are well-made and highly polished.

Her husband, Wallace Youvella, is also a potter, but hasn't had the time to make pottery lately. He is a member of two school boards and told me he was going to give up one of them so he could make pottery. He makes some pieces that resemble Thomas Polacca's work but they are twelve or more inches across with both incising and carving.

Iris signs her work "Iris Y. Nampeyo". Her husband signs "Wallace Youvella". They have two sons, Nolan and Wally, who are also potters.

Pot by Iris Y. Nampeyo

There are many potters on the First Mesa who do beautiful work in the traditional way including Rondina Huma, Susie Youvella (mother of Wallace), Marcia Fritz, Antionetta Silas, Loretta Silas and Venora Silas.

*Deceased

NP=non-potter

Fannie Polacca *

Nampeyo Chart #2

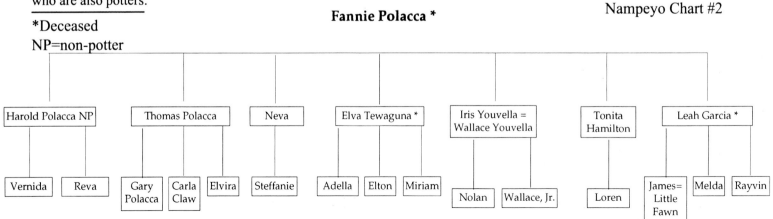

- Harold Polacca NP
  - Vernida
  - Reva
- Thomas Polacca
  - Gary Polacca
  - Carla Claw
  - Elvira
- Neva
  - Steffanie
- Elva Tewaguna *
  - Adella
  - Elton
  - Miriam
- Iris Youvella = Wallace Youvella
  - Nolan
  - Wallace, Jr.
- Tonita Hamilton
  - Loren
- Leah Garcia *
  - James= Little Fawn
  - Melda
  - Rayvin

DEXTRA QUOTSKUYVA

Dextra is famous for her medium to large pots. She uses the Nampeyo designs as well as her own, which come from dreams. Her daughter, Camille (Hisi), often works with her mother. Camille is a young woman with much experience as a potter. She grew up with it. Dan Namingha, the famous artist, is Dextra's son. He attended the American Institute of Indian Arts and lives in Santa Fe.

Pots by Dextra Quotskuyva

Pottery, clockwise, upper left: Jar by Rondina Huma; piki bowl by Myrtle Young; seed bowl and wedding vase by Dextra Quotskuyva; painted redware bowl by Beth Sakeva
Photo by Murrae Haynes

Pot by Steven Lucas
Courtesy of McGee's Indian Arts,
Keams Canyon, Arizona

Jars by Hisi Nampeyo

PRISCILLA NAMINGHA

Priscilla is one of my favorites. She is noted for her very large pots which are perfectly shaped and balanced. The design is also balanced on the pot. This is very important since she is left-handed and sometimes a left-handed person has a problem with the painting; it will drift to the left, and looks as if it's going to slide off the pot.

Priscilla also makes contemporary pottery. I recently saw one of her wedding vases with a design that looked like a patch-work quilt. She also made a pitcher with ears. She is interesting to visit; besides all the pottery talk, we also shared information about our children and grandchildren. All seven of Priscilla's children are potters.

Priscillas' later work isn't as perfect as it was before her eyesight began to fail her.

Water jug by
Priscilla
Namingha

Wedding vase by Priscella
Namingha Nampeyo
Courtesy of McGee's Indian
Arts, Keams Canyon, Arizona

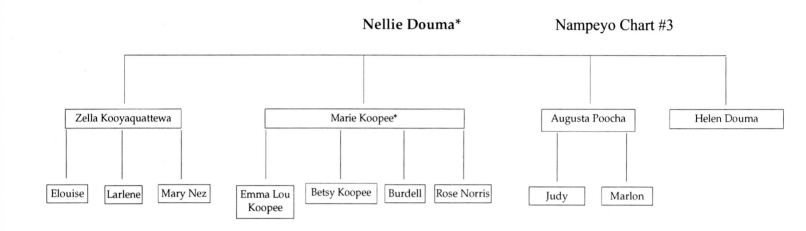

Nellie Douma*   Nampeyo Chart #3

Zella Kooyaquattewa — Marie Koopee* — Augusta Poocha — Helen Douma

Elouise — Larlene — Mary Nez

Emma Lou Koopee — Betsy Koopee — Burdell — Rose Norris

Judy — Marlon

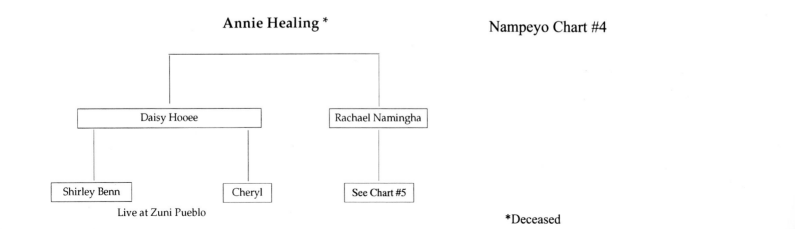

Annie Healing *   Nampeyo Chart #4

Daisy Hooee — Rachael Namingha

Shirley Benn — Cheryl

See Chart #5

Live at Zuni Pueblo

*Deceased

ANDREW AND IDA SAHMIE

Andrew makes pottery whenever he feels like it; I know him best as a kachina doll carver. He married Ida, a Navajo lady, who learned to make pottery from Andrew's mother, Priscilla. So Ida makes Hopi style pottery but uses Navajo designs on them. They are very beautiful and she has won many awards for them. She signs her work "Ida Sahmie" with "Navajo" below her name.

Pot by Ida Sahmie

Rachael Namingha *   Nampeyo Chart #5

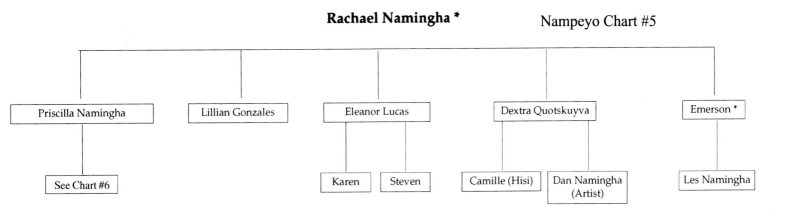

RACHEL SAHMIE

Rachel has been creating some contemporary pottery lately. I have seen a great deal of her work in a showcase at Priscilla's home. While at Keams Canyon Trading Post, I saw several of her pots that were red, small pots with very small designs that covered only a portion of the pot.

RANDALL SAHMIE

Randall Sahmie does unusual things with clay. He makes rattles that are used in Hopi ceremonies. Most rattles are made from gourds, but his are made of clay.

Randall is a woodsman, living a long way from the pueblo. He comes down occasionally into town to pick up supplies.

Priscilla Namingha   Nampeyo Chart #6

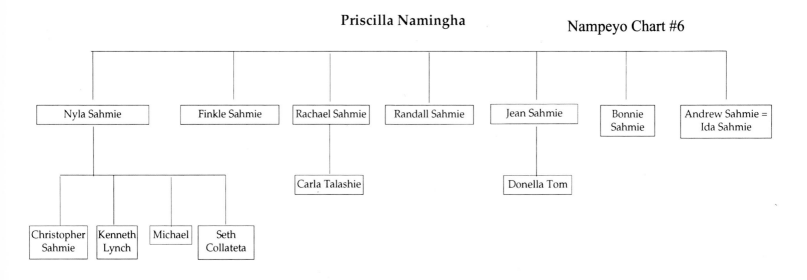

Vase by Loretta Silas

Wedding vase by Venora Silas

Pot by J. Setalla

ISLETA PUEBLO

Isleta is one of the largest pueblos, located south of Albuquerque in the Rio Grande Valley. The small amount of pottery made there is similar to Laguna pottery and often has similar designs. At the time of my visit in the spring, the countryside surrounding the village was beautiful with lush, green pastures and many fruit trees in bloom. The main village has a 700-year history which is very colorful, from its early contact with the conquering Spaniards to its fascinating "ghost story" concerning one of the Spanish priests. An interesting site to visit is the Saint Augustine Mission on the main plaza which is claimed to be the oldest church in New Mexico.

STELLA TELLER

At the age of eight, Stella's mother and grandmother started her in training in the art of pottery making by having her apply the slip and polish the pieces. As her training continued, she learned and formulated her art designs by working on commercial pottery (greenware). By 1963 she was making pottery the old traditional way and now she is the best known of the Isleta potters.

On the day I visited her, she was sanding and polishing figurines. She has developed special tools and methods which allow her to smooth and polish to perfection, even in the smallest areas, before painting. Her jars and pots are as finely finished as her figurines.

Her designs and colors are uniquely her own. She gathers all her raw materials from the Isleta Pueblo. By mixing the colors with the slip, she is able to create the soft, muted colors for which she is well known.

Stella's four daughters are also outstanding potters. Lynette, the youngest, prepares the clay for the entire family, as she is the strongest. For her labor, she receives a commission from the family sales. Stella's granddaughter, Leslie, has continued the family tradition by making pottery in the shapes of small animals.

Stella does her own marketing. Her work can be found in numerous shops and galleries. Some of her work is on display in the Folk Museum in Berlin, Germany.

Stella Teller

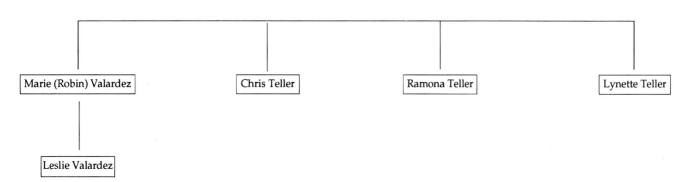

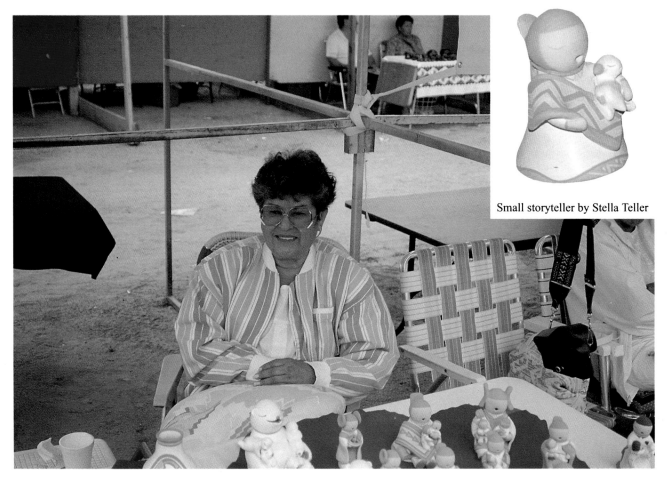

Small storyteller by Stella Teller

Stella Teller and her pottery

JEMEZ PUEBLO

Jemez Pueblo is located fifty miles northwest of Albuquerque. The pueblo dates back to 1703 and has been relocated several times. For three centuries, the Jemez people fought the Spanish to finally settle where they are now. They are the only people who speak Towa. At one time, they painted their pottery with poster paint that was brightly colored and gaudy. Today, their pottery is among the best produced, especially from potters Persingula Gachupin, her daughter Marie Romero, and her daughters, Maxine Toya and Laura Gachupin. I love to visit Jemez because Marie and I have become very good friends.

Pottery, clockwise from left: Three women by Maxine Toya; wedding vase by Juanita Fragua; woman and lamb by Caroline Fragua Gachupin; singing woman by Maxine Toya; sgraffito pot by Glendora Daubs; small jar by Mary E. Toya; canteen by B.J. Fragua
Center: Bowl by Annie and Luisa Panama
Photo by Murrae Haynes

JUANITA FRAGUA

Juanita is best known for her beautiful melon bowls, but she also makes storytellers, wedding vases, nativity scenes, canteens, and all shapes and sizes of jars. The melon bowls are not carved and she pushes the clay out from inside the bowl to form the shapes. Sometimes her wedding vases are done this way on the lower part.

Juanita learned pottery-making from her mother, Rita Casiquito, now in her nineties and no longer making pottery.

Juanita paints the corn design on all her work because she is from the Corn Clan.

The family gets its clay from Jemez and they also dig a black mineral from the earth which they use for black paint instead of using wild spinach, as many other potters do. She tells no one where her source is, for fear that it will be depleted.

When the pots have been polished they are a shiny soft grey. After firing they are a beautiful buff color. Everything is done in the traditional way, except that they fire in a kiln.

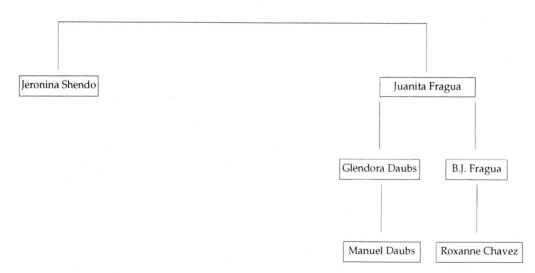

Rita Casiquito

Jeronina Shendo

Juanita Fragua

Glendora Daubs

B.J. Fragua

Manuel Daubs

Roxanne Chavez

Juanita has two daughters who are also outstanding potters. B.J. Fragua also puts the corn design somewhere on all her pottery. She creates her own designs, not copying anyone else's. One design I found especially appealing is the eight-to-ten-inch jar, with carved bands around the top and geometric designs carved and painted within the bands. B.J.'s daughter, Roxanne Chavez, born in 1982, is also making pottery and creating her own designs. She has won several awards for best in her age group.

Juanita's other daughter, Glendora Daubs makes pottery with no resemblance to Jemez pottery. Hers is very finely incised sgraffito. After firing, she carves her designs and the red clay shows through. Glendora likes challenge, and is always coming up with something different. Her work is contemporary, often with stones in the designs. Her young son, Manuel, is also learning. He makes and paints snakes.

This is a talented family. Juanita's son, Cliff Fragua, is a well-known sculptor. His son, North Bear Fragua, is following in his father's footsteps.

Pottery pieces by Juanita Fragua

Pottery by B.J.Fragua

Juanita Fragua family with some of their pottery. Left to right:
Juanita Fragua, Glendora Daubs, and B.J. Fragua
Photo by Murrae Haynes

PERSINGULA GACHUPIN (-1994)

Persingula came from Zia Pueblo and married into Jemez as a young woman. She had grown up with pottery-making at Zia and continued at Jemez. She taught her husband and two daughters, Marie Romero and Lenora Fragua, to make pottery.

Today, Persingula is in her eighties and rarely makes pottery, but occasionally she makes owls. She and Marie were the first in Jemez to make storytellers and nativity sets in the nineteen sixties.

Four generations. Right to left: Laura Gachupin, Damien Toya, Marie Romero, Persingula Gachupin, and Maxine Toya

MARIE ROMERO

Marie is a lady of many talents. She grew up making pottery and because she is from the Corn Clan, all her work has corn painted on it somewhere. She says her family was the first in Jemez to make pottery. She taught pottery-making classes at the Jemez Day School in the late nineteen seventies. Many of the outstanding potters in Jemez were helped and encouraged by Marie.

Marie raised two daughters, Laura Gachupin and Maxine Toya. Marie is also an expert seamstress who makes ribbon shirts and hand-embroidered dresses.

She told me that Laura and Maxine do all the firing outside, at Laura's home. They use cedar wood and Laura always has a good supply. All the pottery is put into metal boxes for the firing.

Marie also has a sister and two nieces who are part time potters.

Sgraffito pot by Marie Romero

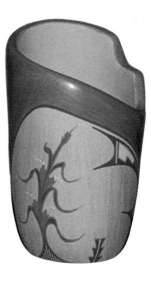

Sculptured pot by
Laura Gachupin

LAURA GACHUPIN

Laura is a versatile potter, always experimenting with the clay. She makes rainbow baskets, storytellers, nativity scenes, and vases with corn appliques and kiva steps. Like the rest of the family, she always puts corn somewhere on her work. Laura has two children, a daughter, Benian, and a son, Gordon. They are learning from the family members and if they continue they, too, will become great potters.

MAXINE TOYA

Maxine is a very busy lady. She is a homemaker, wife and mother, elementary-school teacher, and expert potter. She makes figurines, storytellers, corn maidens, and singing ladies. She shares her art with her students, taking them on field trips to gather clay and other materials needed, and encourages them to make pottery. Maxine makes high quality pottery and wins many awards. She has two children, Damien and Camilla.

DAMIEN TOYA

Damien is a wonderful potter and, like his mother, Maxine Toya, has won many awards. His specialty is the swirled melon bowl and he makes other shapes of pottery also, but the melon bowls are outstanding. He graduated from high school in 1990. He has a great future as a potter.

His sister, Camilla, is working with the clay. Her work is good, and with the encouragement of her mother, grandmother, and great grandmother, she is well on her way.

Persingula Gachupin∗

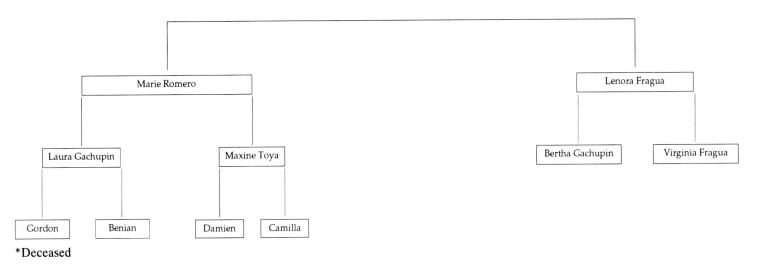

*Deceased

EMILY TSOSIE

It all began with her grandmother, Emilia Loretto, who taught Emily's mother, Grace L. Fragua. Both Emilia and Grace are now deceased. Grace had thirteen children and three of them are deceased. Grace taught Emily to make pottery; Emily made her first storyteller in 1973. She then began to help her mother teach the other children. Some of the younger ones also learned from Marie Romero, a well-known and fine potter, who taught pottery-making to the fifth grade at Jemez Day School.

Emily married Leonard Tsosie who is half Navajo and half Jemez. His mother was a potter and he learned the basics from her. He made pottery sporadically for forty-seven years, but did not become serious about it until he married Emily. Today, he, Emily and their children make their living as award-winning potters. Some of Emily's storytellers have over a hundred children on them. She also makes beautiful corn maidens, Koshari clowns, and Navajo figurines. These figurines are beautifully decorated in traditional dress complete with jewelry and over one arm is a Navajo rug and the other arm is holding a lamb, all done in clay. One of her sisters, Cindy, also makes the Navajo figurines, but she puts a long-horned goat on top of the rug.

Storytellers by
Emily Tsosie

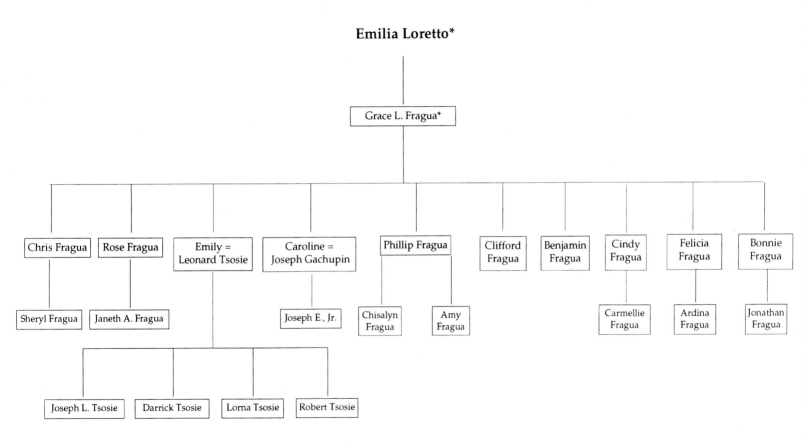

Emilia Loretto*

Grace L. Fragua*

Chris Fragua | Rose Fragua | Emily = Leonard Tsosie | Caroline = Joseph Gachupin | Phillip Fragua | Clifford Fragua | Benjamin Fragua | Cindy Fragua | Felicia Fragua | Bonnie Fragua

Sheryl Fragua | Janeth A. Fragua | | Joseph E., Jr. | Chisalyn Fragua | Amy Fragua | | | Carmellie Fragua | Ardina Fragua | Jonathan Fragua

Joseph L. Tsosie | Darrick Tsosie | Lorna Tsosie | Robert Tsosie

*Deceased

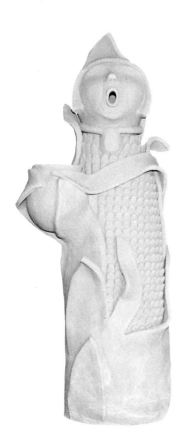

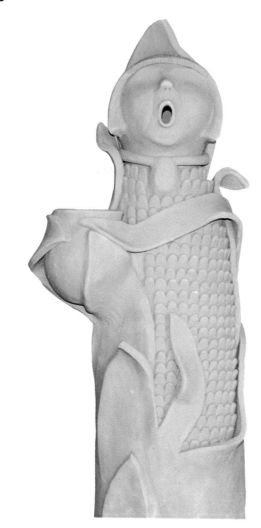

Small corn maiden by Emily Tsosie

Corn maiden, ready to paint, by
Emily Tsosie

Emily and Leonard Tsosie, Storytellers

Emily has nine brothers and sisters who are potters, all making storytellers and figurines and each is outstanding in their work.

Leonard has a daughter from his first marriage who is also a potter. Leonard is now making "grandfather" storytellers with white hair and children from different nations crawling all over him.

Emily and Leonard Tsosie with two of their children, Lorna and Darrick

Showing their storytellers and figures are,
Left: Emily Tsosie with sisters, left to right, Felicia, Rose, and brother Chris;
Rear: Cindy and Bonnie Fragua

Left: Nursing mother by Leonard Tsosie and
Navajo storyteller by Emily Tsosie

Corn maiden by Joseph R.
Gachupin

Storyteller with two children
by Caroline Fragua Gachupin

LAGUNA PUEBLO

The main Pueblo of Laguna may be seen from a pull-off on Interstate 40. An outstanding landmark is the white chapel, built in the late 1800s.

There are approximately 1,895 inhabitants enrolled in this village; three-quarters of these actually live there. There are 6,930 tribal members enrolled, which includes the six Laguna villages as well as satellite villages in New Mexico, Arizona, and California.

Interest in the arts and crafts declined in the middle of the century due to a lack of interest from buyers, but I recently visited Laguna and saw evidence of new interest in pottery-making.

This information was verified by a member of the tribal council office.

Pottery, clockwise from left: Melon bowl, lidded melon bowl, and deer motif jar by Andrew Padilla. Canteen and polychrome jar by Gladys Paquin.
Photo by Murrae Haynes

The Pueblo of Laguna

GLADYS PAQUIN

Gladys Paquin does not have a family tree, really. She and her son, Andy Padilla, Jr., are the only ones making pottery in her family.

Gladys was born at Laguna and is half Zuni, but she was raised at Santa Ana Reservation. After grammar school she was sent to the Indian School in Santa Fe. Eventually she met Andy Padilla from Santa Clara and after they were married they moved to California where her sons, Danny and Andy Jr., were born. Danny, who became a very good potter before he died, signed his work "The Laguna Kid." After Gladys and Andy Sr. were divorced, Andy returned to Santa Clara.

Life became very difficult for Gladys and she turned to Christianity and finally turned her life around. She moved back to her land at Laguna and began to make pottery, but she became very discouraged because she didn't know the traditional designs. Finally, a friend took her to some museums to see old Laguna pots and her friend kept encouraging her. Gladys's pots got better and better and she began to sell them. She was finally on the right track.

She signs her work with her Indian name "SRATYU'WE" and "G. Paquin."

Gladys Paquin firing her pottery the traditional way, outside, with cow manure fuel

Polychrome pot by Gladys Paquin

Opposite page:
The finished pot and proud potter,
Gladys Paquin

ANDREW PADILLA, JR.

Andy, known as "Butch" to his friends, attended high school in Colorado and then returned to Laguna where his mother, Gladys Paquin, taught him to make pottery.

His speciality is melon pots, large and always white. Sometimes he makes them into wedding vases.

Andy married a Navajo lady and lives part of the time at Shiprock, but stays with his mother when making pottery. He signs his work "Andrew Padilla."

Evelyn Cheromiah

Evelyn goes back a long time with pottery in Laguna. The art of pottery almost died out until she got a Federal Grant to teach pottery-making in the village. There were twenty-two students at the first class and half that in the second class. She says they mostly came out of curiosity. Today, not one of the women who attended the classes is making pottery but Evelyn is raising her own group of potters.

Evelyn's daughters Lee Ann and Mary are accomplished potters the traditional way. Her daughter Wendy doesn't make pottery, but her son does, and his pieces are beautiful. He has won several awards. Lee Ann's daughter Brooke is also learning and wants to become a lawyer, so she makes and sells her pots when she needs extra money for school supplies.

Evelyn has kept the traditional pottery-making alive, against all odds. Her beautiful pieces are sought after today across the country.

Evelyn Cheromiah

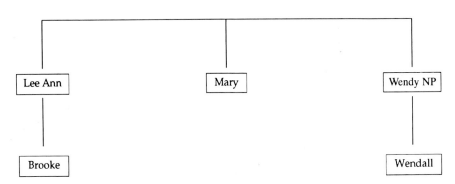

NP=Not a potter

Evelyn Cheromiah and her family

Pottery in different stages by Evelyn
Cheromiah

NAMBE PUEBLO

Lonnie Vigil from Nambe Pueblo makes beautiful micaceous pots.

Micaceous pots by Lonnie
Vigil
Photo by Murrae Haynes

Small bean pot by Priscilla Vigil, large bean pot by Lorencita Pino, Tesuque "rain god"
figurine by an unknown potter
Photo by Murrae Haynes

Picuris Pueblo

The clay from Picuris Pueblo is micaceous (with mica chips throughout) and the pottery made with it is more functional than decorative. Many bean pots are made. The firing method is usually casual in that if there are fire clouds on the pot, the potter likes it that way. Some pots are decorated with a glowing micaceous slip and therefore appear without fire clouds.

Pojoaque Pueblo

Pojoaque is the smallest of the eight northern pueblos. One family of potters at Pojoaque are Joe and Thelma Talachy and their daughter Melissa. Thelma is a sister to Gloria Garcia (Goldenrod), Minnie Vigil and Lois Gutierrez de la Cruz of Santa Clara.

The Talachy pottery is different from any other. Their work is done in black, red, orange and yellow, all colors from the earth.

From this same area, Virginia Gutierrez is noted for her beautiful pottery. Unpolished, but finely and carefully sanded, her seed pots are especially lovely and colorful with designs of animals, kiva steps, feathers, and so may others.

San Ildefonso Pueblo

San Ildefonso is a small pueblo. The Indian name is "PO-WOH-GE-OWEENGE," which means "the water cuts through." The name refers to the place where the Rio Grande runs 24 miles northwest of Santa Fe, New Mexico. The pueblo is beautifully situated on the eastern bank of the Rio Grande, between the Jemez Mountain range on the west and the Sangre de Cristo mountains on the east. The north and south plazas face each other with a huge cottonwood tree on one side.

As I sat on the front porch of his home with Adam (son of Maria Martinez) and his wife, Santana, I commented on the beautiful tree. Adam smiled and said, "My mother watched that tree grow." The land is very fertile and water is plentiful for irrigation for the crops and for the cattle owned by individual ranchers of the Pueblo.

Legends recall that the ancestors of the present-day Tewa were people from the northwest Four Corners area, known as Mesa Verde, where the boundaries of Utah, New Mexico, Colorado and Arizona meet. These people were hunters and farmers.

San Ildefonso was the home of Maria Martinez, who for many years was a great potter. Today, Adam, her only living son, and his wife, Santana, carry on the tradition not only with pottery-making but with helping the Pueblo solve problems and keeping their traditions.

Most of the five hundred residents who are not involved with arts and crafts work in Santa Fe or Los Alamos. San Ildefonso is a beautiful and peaceful place to visit.

San Ildefonso Pueblo

Cottonwood tree on the plaza at San Ildefonso

MARIA AND JULIAN MARTINEZ

Maria Montoya Martinez was in her nineties when she passed away, and what a legacy she left behind! There were many happy times in Maria's life, although she was never happy away from her home. She loved her pueblo life even though there was much grief there as well. Maria and her husband, Julian, worked together until he died in 1943.

Then Maria and her son, Popovi Da, worked together. Popovi Da, a talented man, did the painting and decorating. He and his wife, Anita, had three children: two girls and one son, Tony Da.

Tony set records for his beautiful art work. He was an artist as well as a potter. He experimented with the clay, making many different shapes and sizes, and was using stones in his designs before other potters. I talked with his mother, Anita Da, who owns a little shop and museum on the pueblo. I had heard that he had a motorcycle accident, and was no longer working. Anita said it was a very bad accident and he suffered severe brain damage. Tony remembers nothing of his life be-fore the accident. He is in a nursing home in Louisiana, near one of his sisters, and is presently doing some abstract painting.

Maria's family has experienced joy as well as tragedy. The family tree includes many young potters who learned from their parents and grandparents. They are using designs that are theirs alone, derived from dreams from their young minds as well as the old traditional designs.

Four generations of Maria Martinez family represented by their pottery.
Top: Maria Martinez pot, bear by Adam
Right: Kathy Sanchez
Below: Beaver by Liana

ADAM AND SANTANA MARTINEZ

Adam and Santana Martinez have been inspirational, not only for their family but for all of the pueblo. They set the example for the way things should be. They are never too busy to listen, teach, and encourage anyone who seeks their advice.

Adam Martinez is Maria's only living son. He is in his nineties now and slowing down. Sitting on their front porch, watching the children play on the plaza in front of their home, he spoke of the changes in all of our lives and told stories of how it used to be in the old days.

Adam and Santana still work together making pottery, and many times the grandchildren come to help. Adam gathers the clay and materials and helps with the firing.

Adam and Santana Martinez
and a friend

Pottery, clockwise from left: Jar, ca. 1910, by Maximilliana and Crescencio Martinez;
fish plate and polychrome jar by Maria Martinez and Popovi Da; redware plate by Helen
Gutierrez; blackware jar by Santana and Adam Martinez
Photo by Murrae Haynes

ANITA MARTINEZ (-1992)

Anita Martinez, a daughter of Adam and Santana Martinez, made beautiful black pottery in all shapes and sizes. One of my favorites is the six- or eight-inch lidded black jar without decoration, just plain and highly polished.

Anita's daughters, Kathy Sanchez and Evelyn, gave me the information for the current family tree. When we were finished, they called Anita in from another room and introduced us. She showed me some very old and beautiful pottery made by Maria, Adam, Santana, her children, and some special pieces she had made and wanted to keep for herself.

The Martinez family: Back, Evelyn Garcia, Brandan Gonzales
Sitting left to right: Kathy Sanchez, Santana Martinez, Barbara Gonzales
Kneeling: Berlinda Garcia, Derek Gonzales
Photo by Murrae Haynes

Pot by Kathy Sanchez

KATHY "WAN POVI" SANCHEZ

Kathy is a busy lady who is a well-known potter, home-maker, and educator. She has a B.S. and a Masters degree in education from the University of New Mexico at Albuquerque and taught school for several years on the pueblo.

Kathy is married to Gilbert Sanchez from San Juan Pueblo and they have four talented children, all potters. Gilbert does not make pottery, but he gathers the clay and other materials and assists with the firing.

During the summer months, they travel to shows and give lectures and demonstrations on pottery-making. Kathy always takes pieces to sell which she and her family have made. Kathy's pottery has its own unique look; she makes mostly small pieces and uses the etched and sgraffito technique of decoration which she says is easier than painting. She puts a lot on a pot. A small one with a pitcher mouth has an incised water serpent and a turtle etched inside a sienna colored spot. There is also a bear paw, cactus, mountains, and a feather design and a small piece of coral below the water serpent.

Kathy has won many awards for her pottery. In addition to her responsibilities with her family and pottery, she and others in her family are very active in tribal affairs. They also help Santana with her work.

BARBARA GONZALES

Like her sisters Kathy Sanchez and Evelyn, Barbara Gonzales grew up making pottery. She lived with her great-grandmother Maria Montoya Martinez for several years. Barbara finished elementary school on the pueblo, then was sent to Saint Catherine's in Santa Fe to complete high school. During the summer months she worked on her pottery. She attended the University of New Mexico at Albuquerque for two years, then spent a year at Fort Lewis College in Durango, Colorado.

In 1969, Barbara married Robert Gonzales, also from San Ildefonso, and they have four sons: Cavan, Aaron, Brandon and Derek. She has taught them all to be potters.

One of Barbara's favorite designs is the spider sitting on a delicate silver web. The body of the spider is turquoise. She also makes two-tone black and sienna pots. Barbara does not carve, but she etches her pots and almost always decorates them with inlay stones. Barbara's husband, Robert, is now working with the clay; he makes fetish bears.

Barbara travels to give demonstrations and workshops and has won numerous awards for her work. She is a beautiful young woman with a pleasant personality.

See the following page for family tree.

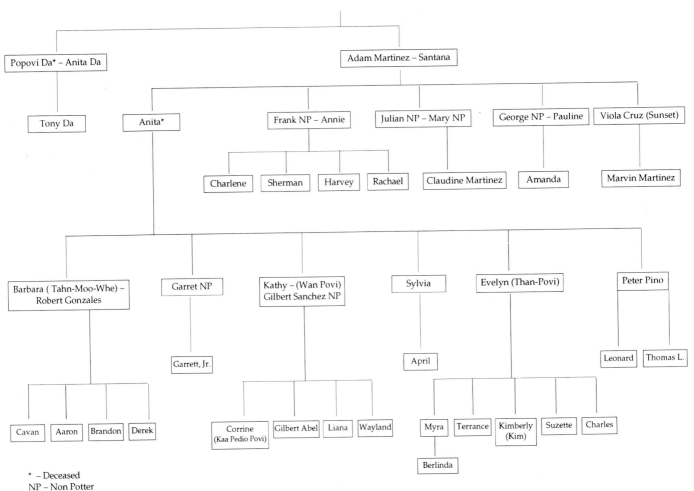

Maria Montoya*   Julian Martinez*

Popovi Da* – Anita Da

Adam Martinez – Santana

Tony Da

Anita*

Frank NP – Annie

Julian NP – Mary NP

George NP – Pauline

Viola Cruz (Sunset)

Charlene   Sherman   Harvey   Rachael

Claudine Martinez

Amanda

Marvin Martinez

Barbara (Tahn-Moo-Whe) – Robert Gonzales

Garret NP

Kathy – (Wan Povi) Gilbert Sanchez NP

Sylvia

Evelyn (Than-Povi)

Peter Pino

Garrett, Jr.

April

Leonard   Thomas L.

Cavan   Aaron   Brandon   Derek

Corrine (Kaa Pedio Povi)   Gilbert Abel   Liana   Wayland

Myra   Terrance   Kimberly (Kim)   Suzette   Charles

Berlinda

* – Deceased
NP – Non Potter

BLUE CORN

Blue Corn is a self-taught potter. She learned by observing, asking questions, and working with the clay. Encouraged by her grandmother, she began potting at the age of three.

She married Santiago Calabaza from Santo Domingo and they returned to her village of San Ildefonso to live. Blue Corn had nine children, seven girls and two boys. As they grew up, they learned to make pottery and helped with the firing. Today, only three of her daughters make pottery on a regular basis. Her son, Craig, gathers all of the clay and materials for his mother and does all the painting of the pottery. Blue Corn makes both red and black pottery and polychrome, which is her favorite .

In front of her home there is a large bird stand where a beautiful macaw lives. A German Shepherd dog is tied to the stand and he does not welcome strangers; it is best to stay in the car until a member of the family comes out to greet you.

Blue Corn gives workshops and demonstrations on pottery-making in several states. She also teaches in the back yard of her home where she is able to include the firing.

Blue Corn – Santiago Calabaza

| Craig | Diane (Sea Shell Flower | Stacey (Roadrunner) | Sophia (Polychrome Flower) |

Pottery by the Martinez family: Top left: Plate by Blue Corn; a bear by
Tony Da Bottom left: Black on black jar and sienna jar by Maria Martinez
and Popovi Da Center: Wedding vase by Gilbert Atencio
Front: Small redware jar by Geraldine Gutierrez
Right: Blackware Kiva by Lucy Martinez
Photo by Murrae Haynes

DORA TSE PE PENA

Dora Tse Pe Pena, originally from the Pueblo of Zia, is the daughter of Candelaria Gachupin, once one of Zia's most outstanding potters. Dora began making pottery at the age of six. She states, "My mother taught me the sacredness of clay, Mother Earth, Father Sun, and Water. All have spiritual significance. My mother taught me that it is very important to know all these things. I treat the clay with much respect. Also, every phase, every step of pottery-making is done only after a prayer and thanksgiving for our gifts: clay, water, fire and artistic talent."

Dora married into San Ildefonso when she married Tse Pe (Juan Gonzales), the son of the late Rose Gonzales, who was a well-known potter in her village. Dora adapted to the different clay by working with Rose, and she learned to carve.

Today, Dora is a full-time potter and makes pottery in- spired by the late Popovi Da. She does the two-color firing, sienna and black, on one pot. She inlays most of her pottery with turquoise and coral stones as well as heishi beads. Dora carves her pots and sometimes uses micaceous clay. Her awards are too numerous to list.

Dora and Tse Pe have five daughters: Irene, Candace, Gerri, Jennifer and Andrea. Jennifer passed away in 1983. Dora and Tse Pe divorced in about 1977. Dora taught all her daughters to make pottery. They each have full-time jobs and make pottery when possible. Irene and Candace are the most dedicated.

Collections of Dora's work are on display in the United States, Guatemala, Switzerland, Japan, China and Germany.

Dora Tse Pe Pena

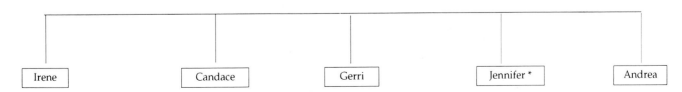

| Irene | Candace | Gerri | Jennifer * | Andrea |

*Deceased

Dora Tse Pe Pena and Irene Tse Pe Pena show their pots.
Photo by Murrae Haynes

San Juan Pueblo

San Juan Pueblo is pretty. There is such a beautiful church in the center of the pueblo and an arts and crafts co-op where lessons are given on pottery making and other crafts.

San Juan clay is reputed to be very hard to dig because there are tree roots growing right where the clay is located. In order to extract the clay, the roots must be cut.

San Juan pottery. Top row left: Bowl by Mary Esther Archuleta
Right: jar with water serpent by Diego and Martina Aguino
Center row left: Jar by Dominguita Naranjo
Center: Jar by Diego and Martina Aguino
Right: Pot ca. 1950, potter unknown
Front row left: carved bowl by Rosita Cata
Photo by Murrae Haynes

DELORES AND ALVIN CURRAN

Delores Curran is from Santa Clara Pueblo and is the sister of Geri Naranjo. Alvin Curran is from San Juan Pueblo.

Delores began potting in the late nineteen sixties, but left pottery for a while, then went back to the clay in the mid-nineteen seventies. She is best known for her miniatures and has won many blue ribbons and prizes for her work. For Indian Market of 1992, she made a larger piece, a lidded jar, eight inches tall. She does not carve, but her pieces are a reddish brown with designs painted in white.

Alvin is also a prize-winning potter. He was taught to make pottery by Delores. Alvin graduated from Espanola High School, then went to college in Monterey, California. He lived and worked in the white man's world for nine years before he returned to San Juan, married Delores, and began making pots. He makes very fine red, carved, San Juan-style pieces.

Delores and Alvin get most of their clay from Santa Clara Pueblo because San Juan clay is so difficult to dig, laced as it is with tree roots.

So far, their daughter, Ursula, shows little interest in making pottery but she is young, and the call of the clay is strong. Her parents hope that after high school, she will go to college, then work outside the pueblo and finally come back home. They want her to understand both worlds, as they do.

Tina Garcia and her blackware pot

Other fine potters in San Juan are Rosita de Herrera and Carnation and Bill Lockwood, a mother-and-son team.

Other potters from Santa Clara, now living in San Juan, are Tina Garcia, Greg Garcia, and Virginia Garcia; a brother-and-sisters team. Their family tree is in the Santa Clara chapter under Severa Tafoya. Their pots are very highly polished, red or black, and sometimes are decorated with the rainbow band. Others are large water jars with scalloped rims.

Dolores and Alvin Curran and pots

Pot by Rosita de Herrera

SANTA CLARA PUEBLO

The Santa Clara Pueblo has a population of 2,600 enrolled members. It is a neat, clean place and pleasant to visit. Legend has it that inhabitants of Santa Clara are descended from the Puye Cliffs (pronounced POO-YAY), which are a famous attraction. There you can see the cliff-dwellings and ruins of long ago. There are some 47,000 acres owned and operated by the tribe, some of it leased to the nearby City of Espanola for businesses.

It is a quiet but busy village. The people take great pride in their homes, and they love flowers. They have summer programs for the children who, at the age of 13, find jobs. They take care of the elders, run errands, clean up, and do anything else that needs to be done. We saw no teenagers hanging around; they were working.

Santa Clara is located along the banks of the Rio Grande and is home to hundreds of potters, many of them descendants of Sara Fina Gutierrez Tafoya. They are known for their creativity, excellence of design, high quality and large quantity of production. Santa Clara potters are credited with the development of black pottery.

Scattered throughout the pueblo are signs reading "Pottery" in front of homes where you are more than welcome to visit. There are also several art galleries exhibiting the products of the Northern Pueblos where the public is always welcomed.

Puye Cliffs

Puye Cliffs

Camilio Sunflower Tafoya (1902-1995)

Camilio, son of Sara Fina Gutierrez Tafoya and older brother of Margaret Tafoya, was born September 15, 1902. In his younger years, agriculture was his main interest. Later he became a renowned potter, but still found time to tend his vegetable and flower gardens.

It has been difficult to write about this family because each one is extremely talented with his and her own style, and their work is exquisite and flawless. Camilio was proud, and rightfully so, of all his children and grandchildren.

Camilio's little gems are carved, showing antelope dancers, water serpents, and other symbols relating to pueblo life. He lived and worked at the home of his son Joseph Lonewolf.

Camilio Sunflower Tafoya and Joseph Lonewolf

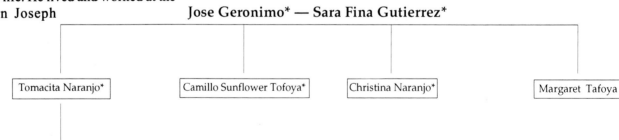

Jose Geronimo* — Sara Fina Gutierrez*

- Tomacita Naranjo*
  - Nicholasa Naranjo
    - Roberta Naranjo
- Camillo Sunflower Tofoya*
- Christina Naranjo*
- Margaret Tafoya

*Deceased

The Camilio Sunflower Tafoya family. Seated left to right: Susan Romero, Rosemary Lonewolf, Lucy Year Flower, Grace Medicine Flower.
Middle: Forrest Tafoya, Kelli Tafoya, Quincy Eagle Feather.
Standing: Adam Speckled Rock, Shawn Tafoya, Myra Little Snow, Gregory Lonewolf
Photo by Murrae Haynes

Pot by Camilio Sunflower Tafoya
Photo by Peter Bloomer, Horizons West

JOSEPH LONEWOLF

Joseph Lonewolf is a man of many talents; woodcarver, jeweler, sculptor, painter, and master potter. He is a true artist. He learned sculpting from his father, Camillio Sunflower Tafoya, and pottery making from his mother, Agapita. Early in his career he made pottery only for his family and friends; he was always searching for different clays and slips.

Using many colors of clay, which he digs in Santa Clara and Colorado, Joseph coils and shapes the clay into round or oval, small and miniature pots. He carves them with a pocket knife. His wildlife scenes are beautifully life-like and flawless. Any imperfect pot is destroyed. They are one of a kind and never duplicated. His works are true "gems of clay."

Prior to his mother's death, Joseph, his wife Theresa, and their three children lived in Colorado where he worked at several different jobs. He visited his mother at Santa Clara to assist her in firing her pots. It was at these times that he learned so much from Agapita. When he returned to Colorado and wasn't working on other jobs, he continued to make pottery. He would visit Santa Clara periodically to fire these pots. He and his wife were divorced soon after their move back to Santa Clara.

Eventually, he met and married Katheryn Favorite who became his business manager so that Joseph could concentrate on his work.

As we sat in their living room, Joseph explained, pointing upward, "He guides my hand as to what I put on the pot. I have visions, and when they fade I go to another pot and He guides me." He may have as many as one hundred-thirty pots on the shelf in various stages of completion. It can often take two years or longer for him to complete a pot. When they are finished, they are signed, numbered, and fired outside. After they are carefully inspected and recorded, they are ready for a collector to treasure forever.

Joseph Lonewolf, 1982
Photo by Katheryn Favorite

Pottery by Joseph Lonewolf
Photo by Peter Bloomer, Horizons West

GRACE MEDICINE FLOWER

Grace Medicine Flower is the daughter of Camilio Sunflower and Agapita Tafoya and the sister of Joseph Lonewolf. Like all her family, Grace has almost always worked with clay. Her first pieces were carved pots and animals. When she became seriously involved with pottery around 1969, her pieces were signed "Grace Hoover." Later, she signed them "Grace" with a four-petal flower. Recent pieces are signed "Grace Medicine Flower" with a flower beneath her name.

Most of her pieces today are commissioned, large, red, carved pots. She is a beautiful lady and her work is very beautiful.

Pottery by Grace Medicine Flower
Photo by Peter Bloomer, Horizons West

Grace Medicine Flower

SUSAN ROMERO

Susan Romero is the daughter of Joseph and Theresa Lonewolf; it was natural for her to become a potter. Her husband, Mike Romero, is an artist and they work together on her designs which sometimes are very complex. She uses a lot of Mimbres figures joined together, completely surrounding the pot from top to bottom. On other pots she carves animals, butterflies, and other natural scenes.

Susan's Indian name is "Pho-Se-We," which means "snowflake." She signs her pottery with a snowflake and "Pho-Se-We." Her exquisite work can be found in better galleries across the country.

Pottery by Susan "Snowflake" Romero
Photo by Peter Bloomer, Horizons West

Susan "Snowflake" Romero

GREGORY M. LONEWOLF (1952-)

Gregory, son of Joseph and Theresa Lonewolf, was born in June 1952 in Fort Carson, Colorado. He studied Police Science at New Mexico University and graduated from the Federal Police Academy in Brigham City, Utah.

Gregory is much involved in the Espanola Valley community, which includes the Santa Clara Indian Pueblo where he lives. He is currently with the city of Espanola Fire Department which also serves both Santa Clara and San Ildefonso villages.

Because of his love and concern for wildlife, Gregory works closely with Northern New Mexico Raptor Rehabilitation and Education near his home.

After a variety of career influences, he chose to devote his talents to the art of pottery-making and other artistic disciplines. Having no formal education in art was not a problem since he was fortunate to have as his teachers his family of famous potters: grandfather Camilio Sunflower Tafoya; father Joseph Lonewolf; Aunt Grace Medicine Flower; sisters Rosemary "Apple Blossom" and Susan "Pho-se-We" Romero.

All their pottery making, including Gregory's, follows the same traditions incorporating delicate, bold, and expertly incised animals, birds, and fish. They are exquisite miniatures.

Gregory's work can be found in numerous galleries and shops across the country.

Gregory Lonewolf

Pottery by Gregory Lonewolf
Photo by Peter Bloomer, Horizons West

ROSEMARY LONEWOLF

Rosemary "Apple Blossom" Lonewolf brings a contemporary style and grace to her pottery that is unique to this family. Her style has taken traditional techniques beyond the southwest market and extended this art-form to those around the world who appreciate fine pottery.

Winner of numerous distinguished awards, and endowed with a legacy of internationally recognized talent, she continues to produce high quality in all her work.

When Rosemary was married to Paul Speckled Rock, they had a son, Adam. He is now a student at the University of New Mexico in Albuquerque. Adam is also an award-winning potter, but now that he is in college he only makes pottery on commission basis.

Currently, Rosemary is married to Louis Baca, a non-potter. His job takes him to many places so I interviewed Rosemary by mail.

Rosemary Lonewolf
and her son Adam
Speckled Rock
Photo by Louis Baca

Pottery by Rosemary "Apple Blossom" Lonewolf
Photo by Peter Bloomer, Horizons West

Pottery by Adam
Speckled Rock
Photo by Peter Bloomer,
Horizons West

LUCY YEAR FLOWER

Lucy is from the pueblo of Pojaque, but in 1957 she married Jose Luis Tafoya, son of Camilio, and moved to his home in Santa Clara. Her pottery career began while she was having coffee with Camilio and watching him work with the clay. He encouraged her to "play" with the clay. She formed a small pot. While Lucy was looking at it and discussing it, her small child jerked on her sleeve and Lucy dropped the pot. It flattened when it hit the floor. After a discussion, Camilio suggested she make it into a whale. It was her first piece of pottery, and today it is in the collection of her sister-in-law, Grace Medicine Flower.

For the next few years, Lucy made small animals. In 1972 she began making larger pieces and carving low-relief designs. She has taught all her children to make pottery. Lucy signs her work "Lucy Year Flower/Pojaque/Santa Clara."

The family tree shows how each potter signs their work.

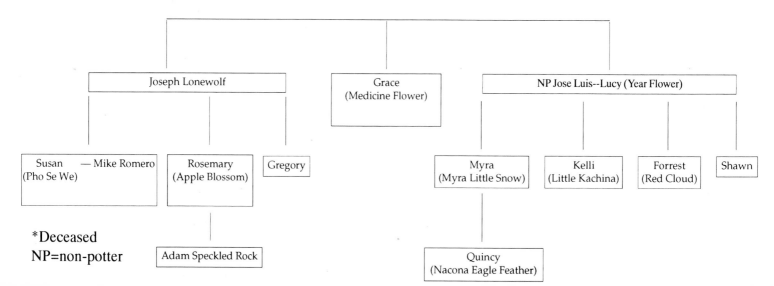

Lucy "Year Flower" Tafoya and family

Myra "Little Snow" Tafoya

Kelli "Little Kachina" Tafoya

NICHOLASA NARANJO

Nicholasa Naranjo's mother, Tomasita, was Margaret Tafoya's oldest sister. Nicholasa is famous for her fine wedding vases and other black pieces. Today, her eyesight is poor so her daughter, Roberta, makes most of the pottery with some help from Nicholasa. Roberta signs her mother's name on the pottery, because she wants her mother to have the credit.

During our interview, it was suggested that they both sign the pots so the public would become familiar with Roberta, and know this was her work, also. The latest pots on the market are signed "Nicholasa and Roberta".

Wedding vase by Nicholasa and Roberta Naranjo

Nicholasa and Roberta Naranjo

TERESITA NARANJO (1917-)

Teresita, daughter of Christina Naranjo and younger sister of Mary Cain, was born in 1917. Teresita makes large, medium, and miniature carved pieces, using the bear-paw and water-serpent designs primarily, in both red and black.

In honor of her beautiful work, she was invited, along with other potters, to the White House in Washington, D. C. during the Nixon Administration.

On large pots, she signs her full name and her Indian name, "Apple Blossom". On the miniatures she puts only her initials, "T.N."

Teresita has three daughters, but only Stella Chavarria is a potter today. Having learned from her mother, Stella does excellent carving and polishing. She, in turn, has taught her daughters, Denise Chavarria and Loretta Sunday, the art. Stella has a little granddaughter, Merissa, who has taken to the clay and, in 1990, won a First and a Third Place at the Indian Market in Santa Fe, New Mexico.

Denise Chavarria pots full-time for a living. She makes small to medium carved pots and her polishing is outstanding. She has three children learning to pot: a son, Paul; a daughter Alisha who signs her work "Lee"; and daughter Danielle who signs her work "Boots."

Loretta holds a full-time position at Los Alamos Scientific Laboratory, but still finds time to make pottery. Her work is very similar to that of her sister, Denise.

Teresita Naranjo

Denise Chavarria

GRACIE NARANJO

Gracie Naranjo is a Navajo lady who married Edward Naranjo, son of Christina Naranjo and the brother of Teresita Naranjo and Mary Cain. Gracie is self-taught, and has been encouraged by her potter friends in the Pueblo. Because of her Navajo beliefs, Gracie does not carve the bear paw or water serpent. Her own designs are beautiful.

Lucy Year Flower is Gracie's strongest supporter, and gives her encouragement.

Gracie's polishing is unbeatable. There is never a polishing stone mark, only a mirror finish.

Edward and Gracie have three children who have learned potting. Edward Jr. is also an accomplished artist in watercolor, oil, and acrylic.

Gracie Naranjo

Mary Louise Eckberry

Mary Louise Eckberry lives in the home of her late mother, Christina Naranjo. She is a spirited and happy person, and a delight to visit. She left Santa Clara in 1946 to be married and lived in Indianapolis, Indiana. While living in Indiana, she made pottery only when she came home for visits. After her husband passed away, she moved back to Santa Clara with her two children, Darlene and Victor. She took care of her mother at the end of Christina's life.

Mary Louise makes and carves traditional Santa Clara pottery. She had no trouble starting up again when she returned to Santa Clara. Both of her children also are potters.

Mary Louise Eckberry

MIDA TAFOYA

Mida is another of the six talented children of the late Christina Naranjo. They were all taught pottery-making by their mother, and they all worked together, helping each other perfect their art. Today, they are all prize winning potters.

Mida carves all her pottery, using the water serpent. She makes both large and small pots. The sanding bothers her, because of the dust, so she must wear a mask.

Mida has seven children, all potters taught by her. Her daughter "Cookie" lives in Nambe Pueblo and has a gallery there. Cookie's son, Maurice, stays with Mida most of the time. Mida taught "Mo," as she affectionately calls him, how to pot, sand, and fire his pottery. He is young but already has won ribbons for his age group.

Mida Tafoya with a pot ready for sanding

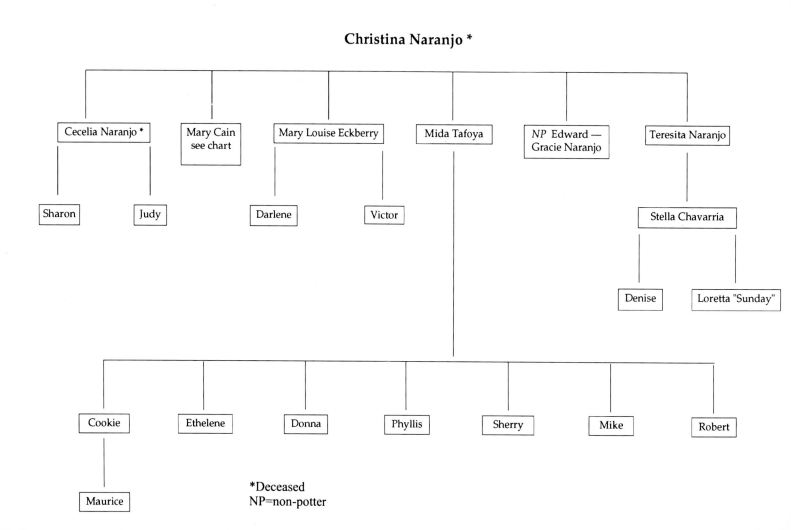

Christina Naranjo *

- Cecelia Naranjo *
  - Sharon
  - Judy
- Mary Cain see chart
- Mary Louise Eckberry
  - Darlene
  - Victor
- Mida Tafoya
  - Cookie
    - Maurice
  - Ethelene
  - Donna
  - Phyllis
  - Sherry
  - Mike
  - Robert
- NP Edward — Gracie Naranjo
- Teresita Naranjo
  - Stella Chavarria
    - Denise
    - Loretta "Sunday"

*Deceased
NP=non-potter

MARY CAIN (1915-)

Mary Cain is another daughter of the late Christine Naranjo and was born in 1915. At an early age, Mary learned to make pottery by watching and helping her mother.

Today, Mary has seven children of her own and several grandchildren, even great-grandchildren, all of whom are potters. Her daughter, Marjorie, lives in California and makes pottery when she comes home for a visit. A granddaughter, Rosemary, attends college in Santa Cruz, California, and occasionally pots during summer vacation.

The rest of the family live nearby and are always dropping in for a visit and to fire their pottery. Tammie Garcia, a granddaughter, lives in Taos, New Mexico and has a gallery there.

Mary Cain and her family make award-winning pottery, both red and black.

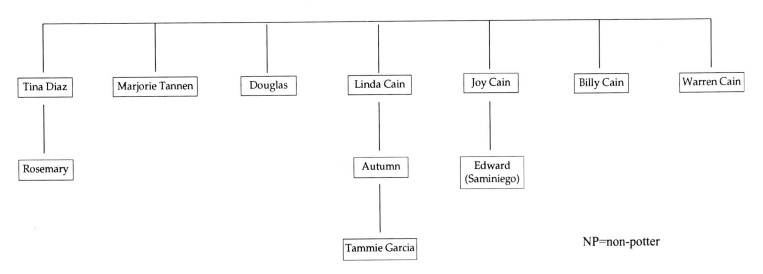

Mary Cain — Willie Cain *NP*

- Tina Diaz
  - Rosemary
- Marjorie Tannen
- Douglas
- Linda Cain
  - Autumn
    - Tammie Garcia
- Joy Cain
  - Edward (Saminiego)
- Billy Cain
- Warren Cain

NP=non-potter

Mary Cain family. Left to right: Autumn Bortz, Tammie Garcia, Linda Cain, Mary Cain, Joy Cain, Tina Diaz.
Back Row, left to right: Edward Samaniego, Billy Cain
Photo by Murrae Haynes

CORN MOQUINO

In 1962, Corn Moquino moved to Santa Clara and married Christine Herrera in 1963; she is not a potter. Corn is self-taught through reading books on the subject, watching and talking to Santa Clara potters. He began to make pots in 1978. Some of his pottery is distinctive because he incorporates Zia, Hopi and other Indian designs incised on Santa Clara style pottery. He signs his work "Corn Moquino."

Today, he has eight sons and one daughter, all of whom make pottery. He maintains a gallery in Santa Clara only for his family's pottery.

Pot by Corn Moquino

Corn Moquino

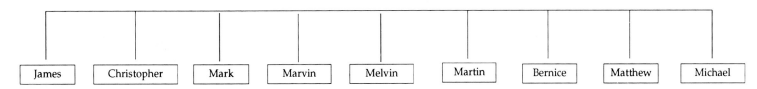

| James | Christopher | Mark | Marvin | Melvin | Martin | Bernice | Matthew | Michael |

Corn Moquino with some of his awards

MADELINE NARANJO

Madeline Naranjo is a soft-spoken, gentle lady. Most of her pottery is black and she is best known for engagement baskets and wedding vases.

She learned to make pottery while living with one of her aunts. Her carved designs are derived from whatever is happening at the time she is carving; if it is a cloudy day, she carves clouds; if it is raining, she carves rain; or whatever comes to her mind.

She has won numerous awards at the New Mexico State fair. From 1976 through 1982 she won five First Place, three Second and four Third Place awards at the Santa Fe, New Mexico, Indian Market.

Her three children and several grandchildren are also award-winning potters.

Madeline Naranjo with one of her pots; only the rim is polished

Madeline Naranjo

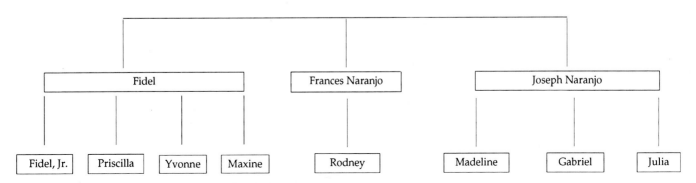

EUGENE GUTIERREZ

Eugene Gutierrez is a versatile potter who alone makes eagle, ram, and buffalo dancers from clay. He was inspired while watching the dances or performing in them. They seem almost to come alive. His parents, Victoria and Celestino Gutierriz, were both potters and he learned from them. He asked a lot of questions and listened to their conversations while they were working.

Eugene also makes the black-on-black pottery and does an outstanding job polishing. He has won many First Place awards, including those given by the Santa Fe Indian Market, the Eight Northern Indian Pueblos Arts and Crafts show, and the New Mexico State Fair.

Eugene is a quiet and easy-going young man who has a promising future as a great potter.

Effie Garcia, seated, with her brother Eugene Gutierrez and Sally Tafoya

EFFIE AND ORVILLE GARCIA

Effie Garcia and her husband, Orville, carve deeper than anyone else I know of at Santa Clara. They are very precise and use jewelers screwdrivers to carve out the designs.

Orville digs and prepares the clay and shapes the pots. They both sit at the kitchen table and carve. Effie does all the polishing and they do the firing together.

Effie and Orville both came from pottery families. Effie is the daughter of Victoria Gutierrez and the granddaughter of Rosita Velarde. Orville is from Acoma Pueblo where his grandmother was a potter, so he grew up watching her. He worked at the uranium mines at Grants, New Mexico before he met and married Effie and moved to Santa Clara. Now they make their living with their beautiful pottery.

Effie Garcia carving

CAROL VELARDE

Carol Velarde has been a potter for more than twenty years. She learned from her mother, Teresa Gutierrez, and her grandmother, Rosita Velarde.

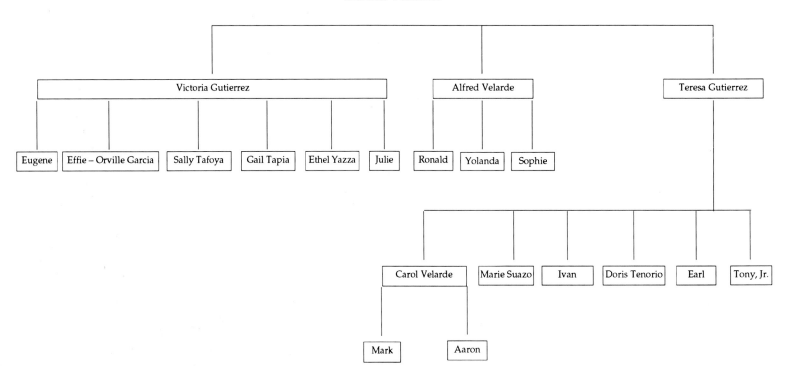

Carol's pots are small and deeply carved. They are carved on a smaller scale than are her cousin Effie Garcia's pieces. Carol draws the outline before she begins to carve. The carvings are deep and delicate. This is a family trait. All members of her immediate family carve the same way and they are active potters. All have won many awards for their pots.

If you look at the work of Carol, her mother Teresa, and her sister Doris Tenorio, you can't tell one from the other since they are so much alike. All three potters are award winners.

Carol's two sons, Mark and Aaron, also are potters. She also has a four-year old son who likes to play around with the clay so Carol helps him shape animals and he spends many happy hours polishing along with his mother.

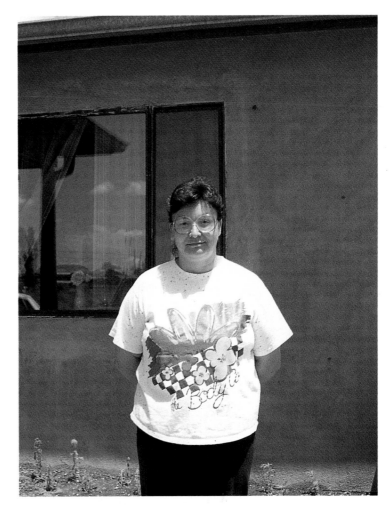

Carol Velarde

ANGELA BACA (1927-)

Angela Baca was born in 1927. The daughter of the late Severa Tafoya, who was a prolific potter, Angela learned from her mother. Today, her specialty is making melon pots.

She entered her pots for the first time in competition at the Indian Market in Santa Fe in 1969 and won First Place awards. She has been commissioned to make some pots for the new Native American Crafts exhibit at the Smithsonian Institution in Washington, D.C.

Angela's children, David, Alvin, and Leona, also make pots. Another son, Darryl, has a full-time job and only pots occasionally.

Pottery, clockwise from left: Polychrome by Lois de la Cruz; early twentieth century blackware, unknown potter; redware with fluted rim by Virginia Garcia; contemporary vase by Jody Folwell; bear paw vase by Severa Tafoya
Photo by Murrae Haynes

Angela Baca

RAY TAFOYA, KENNETH TAFOYA, AND PAUL TAFOYA

While the majority of pueblo potters are women, these three brothers are "the men of the clay," and they each are excellent potters. They are the nephews of Angela Baca and the sons of Tonita Tafoya.

Paul Tafoya changed his name to his Indian name "Speckled Rock" before his marriage to Rosemary Lonewolf (see section on Rosemary Lonewolf). He began making pottery in 1983. The following year he was awarded First, Second and Third prizes at the Gallup Inter-Tribal Ceremonial in Gallup, New Mexico. His other artistic abilities include painting in acrylic, water colors, and pen and ink. He also does sculpting. He owns Merrock Gallery in the center of the pueblo, and is best known for the fetish bears, with bundles of colorful feathers on their backs.

Kenneth Tafoya and Ray Tafoya also have a gallery, next door to Paul's. They all carry their own work as well as the work of other artists in the area, including those from Jemez Pueblo. Ken is a very meticulous artist. He has one piece that he has been working on for over two years. Before it is finished, it will have been fired five times. Each time it is fired, there is a chance that it won't survive. He showed the piece to us and I thought it was beautiful the way it was. He explained that he wanted to add some different colors of slip and turquoise stones before it is finished. Ken proudly showed us some beautiful black pottery his grandmother, Severa Tafoya, had made a number of years ago. One of them still had a price sticker of forty dollars on it. Today, a pot that size and quality would bring six hundred dollars or more. It is not for sale, but is his to treasure.

Ray Tafoya is the most prolific of the three brothers. His small egg-shape pots are colorful, with different colors of clay forming birds, butterflies and other subjects from nature. Clay comes in many colors which they know how to find so the brothers take only what they need; they respect and protect the clay.

Ray is the father of five children, including a set of twins. His wife, Emily, helps him with the pottery and they are teaching the children.

All three brothers fire in a kiln most of the time. These young men are most pleasant to talk to and are eager to answer any questions about their pottery and their families of potters.

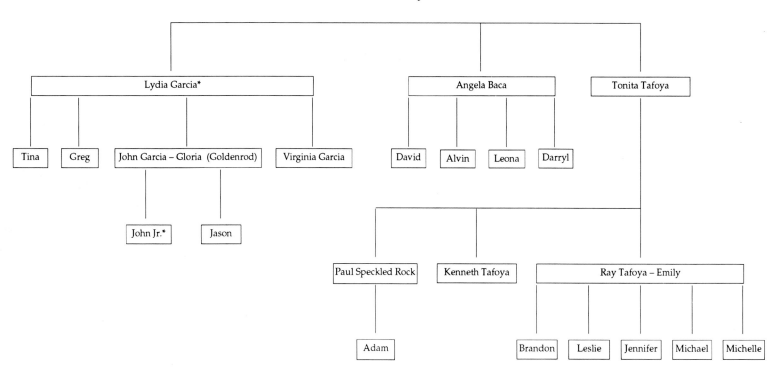

Severa Tafoya*

Lydia Garcia*

Tina | Greg | John Garcia – Gloria (Goldenrod) | Virginia Garcia

John Jr.* | Jason

Angela Baca

David | Alvin | Leona | Darryl

Tonita Tafoya

Paul Speckled Rock | Kenneth Tafoya | Ray Tafoya – Emily

Adam

Brandon | Leslie | Jennifer | Michael | Michelle

*Deceased

Hummingbird pot by Ray Tafoya

Left to right: The three brothers Kenneth Tafoya, Ray Tafoya, and Paul Speckled Rock

Gloria (Goldenrod) Garcia

Gloria Garcia learned to make pots from her mother, Petra Gutierrez, who married into Santa Clara Pueblo from Pojoaque. Petra no longer makes pottery.

Gloria is a contemporary potter, using nature to inspire her designs which include images of trees, animals, and clouds; in fact, anything from nature. She began potting around 1974 and uses a steel-pointed blade to carve. Sometimes she uses coral and turquoise in her designs.

When I ask Gloria's husband, John Garcia, a son of Lydia Garcia, if he also was a potter, he replied, "No, but I help gather the clay, prepare and mix it, help with the designs and fire the pots." Gloria laughed and said, "He does all the dirty work."

They had a son, John David Jr., who passed away in 1991, at the age of twenty-three; he was a potter. Another son, Jason, at age eighteen is showing great promise. Jason makes nativity scenes and other figurines. Most impressive are his sets of Indian dancers on which every detail of the full, colorful costumes is perfect. He made an eight-piece set of the cloud dancers to enter in the competition at the Indian

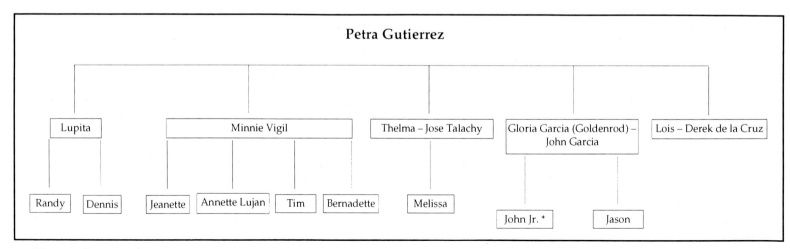

Petra Gutierrez
- Lupita
  - Randy
  - Dennis
- Minnie Vigil
  - Jeanette
  - Annette Lujan
  - Tim
  - Bernadette
- Thelma – Jose Talachy
  - Melissa
- Gloria Garcia (Goldenrod) – John Garcia
  - John Jr. *
  - Jason
- Lois – Derek de la Cruz

*Deceased

Market in Santa Fe. This is a very close family that works on their pottery from start to finish with help and encouragement for each other.

Gloria's large family includes many potters. Her sister Minnie Vigil makes small pots with painted designs. Another sister Lois Gutierrez makes large and beautifully painted polychrome pots. She and her husband, Derek da la Cruz, work together on her pots.

Jason Garcia and his mother
Gloria "Goldenrod" Garcia

Lois de la Cruz Gutierrez

Cloud dancers by Jason Garcia

STEPHANIE NARANJO (1960-)

Stephanie Naranjo and her great aunt, Margaret Gutierrez, are still carrying on the tradition of making pottery like that made by Stephanie's great grandparents Van Gutierrez and Lela Naranjo. They are the only ones who do the whimsical figurines. After Van and Lela passed away, their son and daughter, Margaret and Luther Gutierrez, picked up their parents' technique.

Margaret Gutierrez began making pottery when she was very young. She became as skilled as her mother. Margaret made the pieces and Luther painted designs on them. After Luther passed away, Margaret and Stephanie took over the work. They often work together, and always do the firing together.

Stephanie was born in 1960 and began making pottery at the age of 8. After high school, she attended Santa Fe College and received a degree in art.

*Deceased

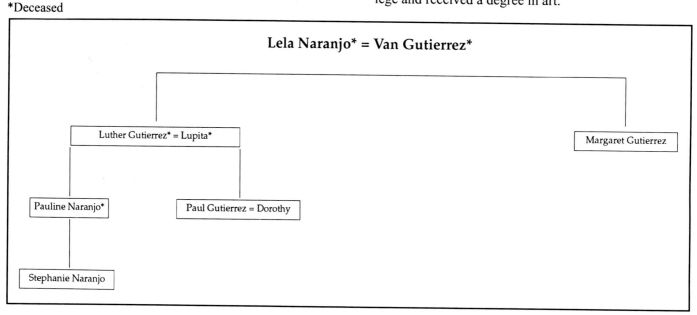

Lela Naranjo* = Van Gutierrez*

Luther Gutierrez* = Lupita*

Margaret Gutierrez

Pauline Naranjo*

Paul Gutierrez = Dorothy

Stephanie Naranjo

Other members of the family who make figurines are Luther's son Paul Gutierrez and his wife Dorothy. They make mud-head storytellers and figurines which are a matte-black, with polished mouths, ears, and top-knots.

Stephanie Naranjo

Turtle by Stephanie Naranjo

Margaret Gutierrez

Pottery, clockwise from left: Blackware jar by Greg Garcia; carved redware by Lagoria Tafoya; wedding vase by Elizabeth Naranjo; polychrome jar by Margaret and Luther Gutierrez; carved blackware by Madeline Naranjo; melon pot by Angie Baca; polychrome by Belen Tapia
Photo by Murrae Haynes

CRESENCIA TAFOYA

Cresencia Tafoya has been making traditional black Santa Clara pottery for many years. She sells from her home studio.

Cresencia raised six children and taught each of them to make pottery at an early age. Harriett makes mostly small jars, both red and black. She doesn't carve, but does the black-on-black painting. Her polishing is excellent with a mirror finish. She stopped making pottery for almost a year because her only child, a son, Ivan Red Starr, was killed by a car the summer of 1991. He was only twenty-two years old and had showed great promise as a potter. Harriett is trying to get her life together and has begun to make pottery again.

Cresencia's daughter Annie Baca is a well-known potter. She does some carving, but mostly she does black-on-black painted pots.

Another daughter, Pauline, married George Martinez, the son of Adam and Santana Martinez of San Ildefonso Pueblo. Pauline and George live in San Ildefonso and make black-on-black pottery, which is predominate at that pueblo.

Cresencia's three other children, Arthur and Mark Tafoya and Carmen Michel, carve both red and black pottery.

*Deceased

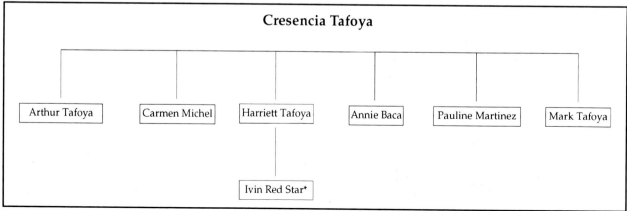

Harriet Tafoya

Fetish bear by Red Star, a Sioux living at Santa Clara

Annie Baca

GERALDINE (GERI) NARANJO

Geraldine Naranjo began making pottery at an early age, around eleven years old, after being taught by her mother, the late Ursulita Naranjo. Making pottery was a hobby for her at first but, as time went by, she became seriously interested in making miniatures. Not many of her perfect little vases and bears are over two inches tall. She signs all of her work simply "Geri," because they are so small.

Geri's son, Kevin, and daughter, Monica, are also award-winning potters.

Geri Naranjo

*Deceased

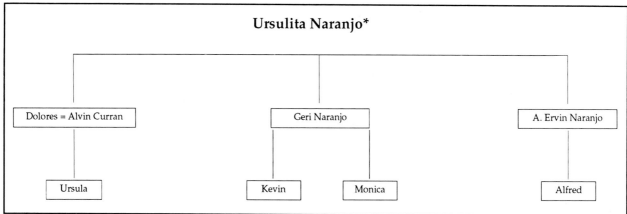

MARGARET TAFOYA'S FAMILY

Margaret Tafoya's large family of potters objects to kiln firing as opposed to the traditional method of firing pottery outside in a natural fire. The entire family fires in an outdoor fire, which they feel is the true method of firing Pueblo pottery. They do not feel that anything is wrong with kiln-fired pottery, but it must be represented as such. Also, there are many at Santa Clara who purchase ceramic ware, paint it black, fire it in a kiln, and sell it as a traditional pot. This family tree is presented to identify these excellent potters who are not related to other Tafoya families. There are many people named Tafoya who live in and around Santa Clara Pueblo.

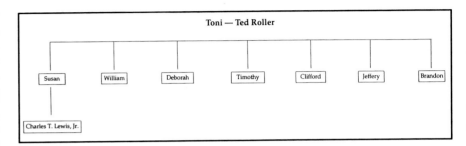

Toni — Ted Roller

Susan · William · Deborah · Timothy · Clifford · Jeffery · Brandon

Charles T. Lewis, Jr.

*Deceased

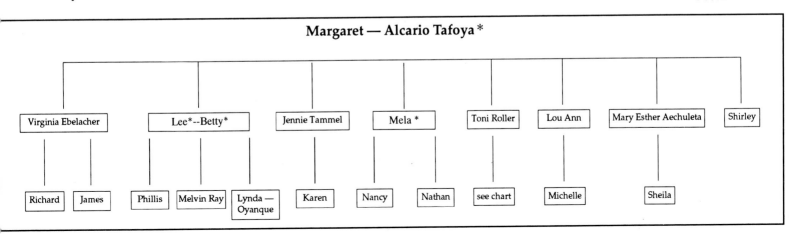

Margaret — Alcario Tafoya *

Virginia Ebelacher · Lee*--Betty* · Jennie Tammel · Mela * · Toni Roller · Lou Ann · Mary Esther Aechuleta · Shirley

Richard · James · Phillis · Melvin Ray · Lynda — Oyanque · Karen · Nancy · Nathan · see chart · Michelle · Sheila

SANTO DOMINGO PUEBLO

Santo Domingo Pueblo is located in northern New Mexico along the Rio Grande just south of Santa Fe.

My research at Santo Domingo Pueblo was a real adventure. I had an appointment for an interview with potter Manuelita Lovato the day after my arrival. There was to be a wedding of her nephew and a huge feast afterwards. We were invited. I knew that the Pueblo would be crowded and I wanted to interview potter Robert Tenorio the day before the feast.

I was taken into the governor's office and the lieutenant governor was brought in. I was interrogated about what I was doing and they wanted to be present when I talked to Robert, in case I asked something about their religion and way of life. I tried to assure them that I was only interested in the pottery making. My husband was outside in the car waiting for me. They asked that I bring him in, which I did. They asked him many questions, too. When I told them that we had been invited to a wedding the following day, the lieutenant governor beamed and said that the bride-to-be was his niece. They both stood up and said "See you at the wedding feast." We had been dismissed!

The following day, the governor and his entourage greeted us warmly. He asked if we had talked to Robert the day before. I replied "No sir, you wouldn't tell me how to find him." He introduced me to Robert and I interviewed him later.

Opposite page:
Pottery clockwise from left: Hispanic jar, ca. 1915, and dough bowl by Santana Melchor; bowl by Robert Tenorio; bowl by Hilda and Arthur Coriz
Photo by Murrae Haynes

MANUELITA LOVATO

Manuelita Lovato is a most remarkable lady. She is a professor at the Institute of American Indian Arts in Santa Fe. She gives lectures, consults, is a regional coordinator for the Four Corners Southwest Area Museum, and is the only practicing Native American conservator. She also has been a museum curator in Colorado.

Besides being a silversmith working with gold, silver, and stones, she is a self-taught potter. She began making pinch pots in 1964 and went on to experiment with different clays on the pottery wheel; then she learned the coil method which she uses today.

Manuelita makes unusual pieces such as bottle shapes with stoppers decorated like jewelry with lacquered brass, coral, turquoise, jet, sugalite, mother-of-pearl, and spiny oyster shell. The bottle part is incised with designs of lizards, spiders, turtles, etc. outlined with small stones. Her pieces are "smoked," as she calls the process, with animal manure before the stones are placed. Manuelita's pieces are not Santo Domingo style. They are one of a kind, her own designs and are unlike anyone else's work.

Her young niece Trudy is learning from Manuelita to be a potter and has won awards for her age group.

Manuelita Lovato holding her pot

Vase by Manuelita Lovato engraved with Mimbres lizard design and with a lacquered brass top inlaid with turquoise, mother-of-pearl, spiny oyster shell, sugalite, and jet

ROBERT TENORIO

In 1968, Robert Tenorio enrolled in the Institute of American Indian Arts in Santa Fe to learn jewelry making. Most of the people of Santo Domingo make jewelry, but Robert was always sneaking into the ceramic class to play with the clay.

He would make stew bowls and ollas for his mother, Juanita Tenorio. At that time, he was using commercial clay and firing in a kiln. Today he uses Santo Domingo clay and traditional firing methods. All his paints are from the earth. Most of his pottery is large and boldly decorated with geometric designs. He says that after the firing he rubs egg-whites or grease on the pots to make them shine.

Robert has won many awards at the yearly Indian Market competition in Santa Fe. His pottery now is sought all over the country and abroad. He is very involved in his community's affairs and devoted to his family, especially his grandmother, potter Andrea Ortiz, who was over one hundred years old when she died in 1993.

My interviews with Robert took place during a wedding celebration at Santo Domingo and later on the telephone. He gave me the information for his family tree and on his work. Robert says that he keeps his prices reasonable because the only thing he has to buy is sandpaper.

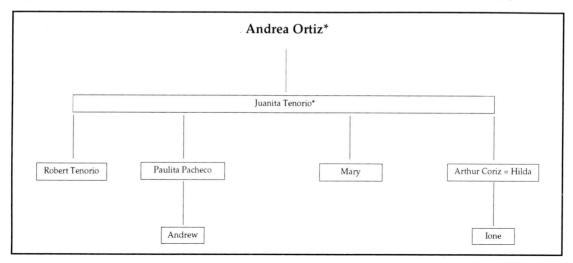

Andrea Ortiz*

Juanita Tenorio*

Robert Tenorio   Paulita Pacheco   Mary   Arthur Coriz = Hilda

Andrew   Ione

*Deceased

TAOS PUEBLO

The Robert Tenorio family. Front row, left to right: Paulita Pacheco, Ione Coriz, Robert Tenorio
Back Row: Mary Tenorio, Arthur Coriz, Hilda Coriz, and Andrew Pacheco
Photo by Murrae Haynes

Clay from Taos Pueblo is threaded with mica chips, called micaceous clay. Pottery made with it is functional rather than decorative, such as bean pots. Because its firing is casually done, there often are fire clouds on the pots which the potter likes. When these pots are decorated with micaceous slip, the fire clouds are hidden.

TESUQUE PUEBLO

ZIA PUEBLO

Tesuque Pueblo, just north of Santa Fe, is the home of the "rain god," so ugly that it is endearing. Renderings of the rain god once were made for the tourist trade, and at one time were given with a box of candy by the Gunther Candy Company.

Zia is one of the oldest pueblos in New Mexico, dating back to the 1300s. There are few active potters there now.

Tesuque Rain God by V. Leno

ELIZABETH AND MARCELLUS MEDINA

The Medina family is the most active making pottery at Zia Pueblo today, and Elizabeth Medina does outstanding work. She was born and raised in Jemez Pueblo and learned to make pottery from her mother, Mary Toya.

Elizabeth Toya married Marcellus Medina from Zia and they established their home at Zia Pueblo. Marcellus' mother, Sofia Pino Medina, is a potter. His father, Rafael Medina, is an artist who also helped Sofia with the pottery-making and firing. Elizabeth worked with Sofia to learn how to use the Zia clay which is different from that of Jemez; Zia clay is tempered with basalt instead of sand.

Elizabeth makes all sizes of pottery from tiny pots to large ollas. She uses the Zia designs, the best-known being the wide-eyed, split-tailed bird. Marcellus is not a potter, but a painter. He paints his wife's plain pots, using acrylic paints. Beautiful eagle, deer, and buffalo dancers come alive in his work. His father taught this art to Marcellus. Rafael doesn't paint anymore because of his poor eyesight, but Sofia still makes the huge ollas. The family works together in their firing.

Kimberley and Marcella are away in school, they are not potters.

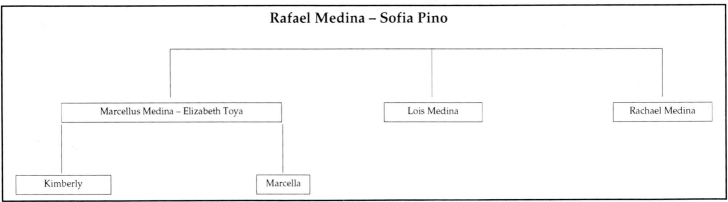

Rafael Medina – Sofia Pino

Marcellus Medina – Elizabeth Toya   Lois Medina   Rachael Medina

Kimberly   Marcella

Marcellus and Elizabeth Medina show their pots
Photo by Murrae Haynes

ZIA SISTERS

Other semi-active potters in Zia Pueblo include three sets of sisters. Eusebia Shije and Teresita Galvin make pottery occasionally. Teresita works at the tribal office and makes pottery on the weekends.

Louise Negal and Florenda Shije make a small amount of pottery.

Dolorita and Pablita Pino also make pottery from time to time. All six of these women do beautiful work and fire in a kiln.

Pot by Eusebia Shije

A Zia pot resting on a drum showing the black bird

ZUNI PUEBLO

Zuni is an ancient pueblo dating back to the 1500s. When there, one must visit the old mission church that was built around 1629 and reconstructed between 1960 and 1970. It was then that Alex Seowtewa began work painting murals inside the church. Alex and his two sons, Edwin and Ken, are still working on the life-size paintings of Zuni Kachinas on the walls of the mission.

Alex and I sat in front of the altar as he told me about the Kachinas and about his talking with several village elders about which Kachinas to paint. He also told me about his trip to Russia, where he studied the old churches, icons, and other works of art.

He was so happy to return to America that he kissed the ground when he landed in Seattle.

His painting is some of the most beautiful art work I have ever seen. The colors are vibrant. The magazine *Native Peoples'* winter 1992 issue has a wonderful article about these murals with pictures. The text was written by Ken Seowtewa.

The old mission at Zuni

After twenty years, the murals are still not completed. The mission church is a wonderful place to visit, to enjoy both the old building and the paintings. A private visit with Alex is definitely an honor.

THE NAHOHAI FAMILY

Josephine Nahohai is the matriarch of this family of potters. They win awards and ribbons at every show they enter. Josephine learned to make pottery by helping an uncle's wife. Josephine learned to make owls first, in about 1969. Her late husband painted her work until his eyesight became too dim, then their son, Milford, took over this chore in addition to making and painting his own pots. Milford doesn't make as much pottery as he would like because he has a full time job as assistant manager of the Pueblo of Zuni Arts and Crafts Shop. He also travels to promote Zuni arts. Now another relative, Dion Nahohai, paints for Josephine. Milford does beautiful work and always has pots around in different stages of completion.

Randy, another of Josephine's sons, is also a potter. He graduated from the Institute of American Indian Arts in Santa Fe, majoring in two-dimensional art. He began his pottery career by painting ceramics and using a high glaze, then fir-

Nahohai family. Front: Josephine and Rowina Back: Milford and Randy

ing in an electric kiln. Today he makes traditional pottery, but sometimes fires in a kiln in bad weather. He almost always takes first place in the Northern Arizona show at Flagstaff, Arizona.

Randy also designs jewelry and T-shirts. His wife, Rowina Him, used to make beaded jewelry, but soon after she married Randy she became a potter because of the influence of his family. Rowina's owl are wonderful, done in the style of Josephine's work. The eyes bulge with lines drawn out from the pupils; they look sleepy.

Josephine has two daughters, Priscilla and Irma, who make pottery, but not on a regular basis.

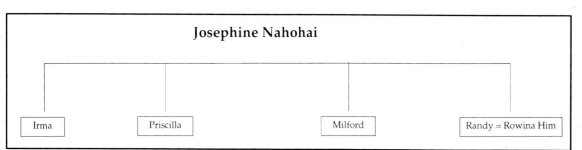

Josephine Nahohai

| Irma | Priscilla | Milford | Randy = Rowina Him |

QUANITA KALESTEWA

Quanita Kalestewa and her husband, Jack, previously made jewelry, but now devote their talents to pottery-making.

Quanita learned to make pottery by watching her mother, Nellie Bica, a well-known Zuni potter, but she showed no interest in the clay until the nineteen-forties. Jack also came from a pottery-making family.

They gather the clay and natural minerals for their paints on the Zuni Reservation, and buy the white clay for slip from Acoma. The thinness and whiteness of their pots make them resemble Acoma pottery, but the designs are all Zuni.

They make owls and corn-meal bowls with both painted and appliqued frogs, tadpoles, lizards, and serpents.

Quanita's mother is elderly now, but with the help of her family, she still produces quality pottery.

This family makes traditional pottery from start to finish.

They fire their pots at their sheep ranch, just outside the pueblo, where they have a good supply of sheep manure for fuel.

Quanita Kalestewa

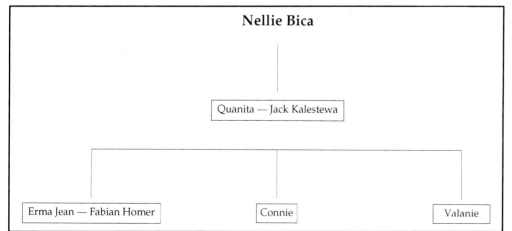

Nellie Bica

Quanita — Jack Kalestewa

Erma Jean — Fabian Homer   Connie   Valanie

Owl and babies by Quanita Kalestewa

Peynetsa Family

Priscilla Peynetsa took a pottery class while in the seventh grade at high school. The classes were taught by Jennie Laate, an Acoma potter who married into Zuni.

These pottery classes were an elective and Priscilla wasn't interested at the time in making a career with pottery. However, sometime later she had an accident and wasn't able to work. During her recovery, she decided that perhaps she could make pottery for a living. Then she started evening pottery classes and took it seriously.

The Peynesta family. Left to right: Aurelia, Anderson, Agnes, and Priscilla

Priscilla's work is distinctive, and once you see it, you know it is Priscilla's. The pots are red with bold, black designs of tadpoles, water serpents, and dragonflies. Sometimes she paints a lizard up to a certain point and then appliques the body. Everything is traditional except that she fires in a kiln unless someone asks her to fire outside, then she gets someone to help her.

Priscilla's brother, Anderson, was the next to come to the clay. He has been potting for over ten years and is best known for making large jars using traditional Zuni designs, especially the "deer in his house" design with the heart-line. Anderson's wife, Aurelia, does the polishing for him. He and Priscilla use similar designs, and sometimes it is difficult to tell them apart until you look at the signatures.

Agnes, their sister, has been potting for about seven years. Her pottery is similar to that of her siblings. Some are small round balls with the serpent encircling the pot in applique. Agnes learned from Priscilla and Anderson. They use traditional methods except that they usually fire the clay in a kiln.

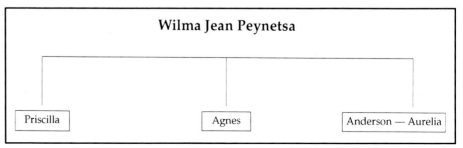

Wilma Jean Peynetsa

Priscilla   Agnes   Anderson — Aurelia

Values Reference

Artist, (alphabetically)	Size	Description	Cost
ACOMA PUEBLO			
B.J. Cerno	1-1/2" x 1-5/16"	Small seed pot, round-white, black and orange mimbres	$100
Peggy Garcia	4-1/2" x 6"	Storyteller, 5 children, Hopi hair design	$225
Carmel Lewis	2-9/16" x 2-3/4"	Black and white lightening design pot	$85
Diane Lewis	1-3/16" x 3-7/8"	Oval, seed pot, Kiva steps carved on top mimbres figure - painted brown, orange & black	$125
Dolores Lewis	1-5/16" x 2-3/4"	White turtle, black circle and cross hatch on top	$75
Lucy Lewis	2-5/16" x 4-1/4"	Black and white, lightening designs	$500
Emma Lewis	1-15/32" x 1-3/8"	Seed pot, black deer mimbres figures	$45
Emma Lewis	1-1/16" x 2-1/8"	Black and white cloud designs, small pot	$40
Thomas Natseway	5/8" x 17/32"	Miniature Kayenta water jar, grey & white designs	$130
Marie Lilly Salvador	5" x 3-1/2"	Migration vase, 4 bands, orange background, mimbres designs	$800
Mary Sanchez	10-3/16" x 10-7/8"	Ola Jar, cross hatch design, flute player on 1 side, sun god on other	$250
Ethel Shields	5-1/2" x 8-1/4"	Dog Canteen - white, black designs	$135
Judy Shields	1-1/2" x 15/16"	Miniature owl storyteller, 4 owls on 1, brown and white	$200
Jackie Shutiva	7-5/8" x 5-1/2"	White corrugated wedding vase, designed stirrup	$150
HOPI PUEBLO			
Clara Claw	1-9/16" x 3-5/8"	Seed pot, dark brown, incised (Nampeyo) hummingbird	$175
Verla Dewakuku	1-1/2" x 3-5/16"	Light brown, geometrical black designs	$50
Verla Dewakuku	2-7/16" x 3-9/16"	Light brown, geometrical black designs	$50
Lejume Havato	1-1/2" x 4-5/8"	Clay pipe, buff and brown designs, water designs	$15
Deidre Johnson	2-11/32" x 2-1/4"	Brown eagle wing designs	$50
I. Namingha	3-1/4" x 4-1/8"	Buff jar, brown and black geometric designs	$50

Artist, (alphabetically)	Size	Description	Cost
Lawrence Namoki	2-7/16" x 2-1/2"	Round pot, carved owl dancer, tan and brown designs	$125
Manayrd & Veronica Navasie	3-3/16" x 5-5/16"	Round pot, white background, brown and tan designs	$275
Rachael Sahmie	1-1/4" x 2-1/16"	Small seed pot, geometrical desings	$50
Loretta Silas	5-1/8" x 5-1/2"	Buff with brown designs, geometric and tadpole designs	$230
Venora Silas	8-3/16" x 5-1/4"	Buff wedding vase, geometric designs in brown and black	$240
Deanna Tahbo	2-1/4" x 2-7/8"	Buff with geometric designs in brown	$45
Diane Tahbo	4-3/16" x 6-1/2"	Round pot, golden brown, dark brown and black designs	$350
Diane Tahbo	9-16" x 3/4"	Miniature tan and brown geometrical designs	$25
Diane Tahbo	11/16" x 1-1/16"	Miniature tan and brown butterfly design	$35
Iris Youvella	2-5/16" x 2-1/2"	Small buff pot, corn applique on one side	$325
JEMEZ PUEBLO			
Chinana	3-13/16" tall	Storyteller, 5 children pot on top of head	$100
Bonnie Fraqua	6-7/8" tall	Storyteller, 5 children, 1 hand over mothers mouth all singing, 2 books	$300
JFG	1-9/16" x 1-5/8"	Seed pot, incised, brown	$25
Laura Gachupin	4-3/4" x 2-7/8"	Red polished vase, kiva step carving, designs painted on buff side of corn stalk and pollen	$150
Marie Romero	6-1/8" x 4-5/16"	Polished red vase, 3 ears corn applique with corn stalk, painted on front	$280
Sabaquie	3-9/16" x 3-3/8"	Seed pot, oval designs, white, red and black	$27
Maxine Toya	7-5/8" tall	Corn maiden, polished sections, hair is done in Hopi style, 3 rows of corn across chest	$675
Emily Tsosie	7-5/8" tall	Navajo storyteller	$500
Emily Tsosie	7-5/8" tall	Storyteller nursing mother	$375
Emily Tsosie	7-5/8" tall	Corn maiden, buff, lots of designs on back rows of corn across chest, red cheeks, black dots around red cheeks	$250

Artist, (alphabetically)	Size	Description	Cost
Carol Vigil	1-1/8" x 1-3/8"	Red seed pot, incised designs	$60

LAGUNA PUEBLO

Artist, (alphabetically)	Size	Description	Cost
Gladys Paquin	6-3/8" x 5-1/2"	Jar, painted red rainbirds and Kiva steps	$150

SAN IDELFONSO PUEBLO - 5 Generations of Same Family

Artist, (alphabetically)	Size	Description	Cost
Adam Martinez	2-7/8" x 5"	Black, polished bear standing on 4 legs	$350
Anita Martinez	2-11/16" x 3-11/16"	Black, polished pot with sienna top	$260
Maria Martinez	2-15/16" x 4-1/8"	Undecorated, highly polished black pot	$1400
Kathy Sanchez	3-13/16" x 3-3/4"	Polished black pot, pitcher opening, piece of inlay coral, incised turtle	$375
Liana Sanchez	1-7/8" x 4-7/16"	Polished black beaver, turquoise stones, eyes and tail	$75

SANTA CLARA PUEBLO

Artist, (alphabetically)	Size	Description	Cost
Denise Chavarria	2-13/16" x 3-9/16"	Black, highly polished, carved shamrock shaped opening at top. Dated 7/91	$160
Tina Diaz	4-28/32" x 4-9/32"	Black, heavily carved black matt paint between	
Gregory Lonewolf	15/16" x 1"	Seed pot, hummingbird incised on top, red, blue, white flowers and feathers. #WGWRMG carving. Water serpent design.	$320 $375
Joseph Lonewolf	1-5/8" x 1-5/8"	Buff background, incised Dahl rams - 1 laying down and 1 standing, butterfly, 1991 peace symbol, blue top, white feathers. #C1WRCW	$2900
Rosemary Lonewolf		5 piece set - miniatures (Apple Blossom) Red and buff, round, blue accents	$575
#1	3/4" x 5/8"	Hummingbird and flowers	
#2	13/16" x 11/16"	Jar, feather designs around tapered top, bottom blue background. Carved water serpent	
#3	5/16" x 13/16"	Flat top pot, fish incised on top, water designs around base	
#4	11/16" x 3/4"	Cone shaped, butterflies and flowers	
#5	5/8" x 7/8"	3-sided piece, incised bug mimbres	
Grace Medicine Flower	1-3/16" x 1-1/2"	Red pot, incised butterfly covering entire top	$950
Corn Moquino	3-3/16" x 2-3/4"	Red and buff, carved buck, doe and fawn deer and trees	$65
Matthew Moquino	1/2" x 1-3/4" x 1-1/8" x 2-1/16"	Turtle, back, grey back, arrow with turquoise stone	$5
Madeline Naranjo	6-15/16" x 4-1/2"	Black, polished engagement basket, water serpent carved	$375
Nicholasa & Roberta Naranjo	9-3/8" x 7-1/2"	Black, polished wedding vase, black on black feather designs	$425
Stephanie Naranjo	2-7/8" x 7" x 5-5/8"	Turtle, grey, mimbres designs on back-open mouth	$250
Teresita Naranjo	1-1/8" x 1-7/16"	Red, carved water serpent	$200
Cliff Roller	2-1/2" x 5-5/16"	Black, polished bowl. Dated 4/91	$450
Susan Romero (Snowflake)	1-11/16" x 1-7/8"	Red seed pot, deer head incised, also geometric figures	$525
Adam Speckled Rock	2-5/16" x 2-5/16"	Red, incised pinto horse with blue sky, mimbres horses all around. J-1	$520
Ivan Red Starr	1-5/16" x 1-5/16"	Artist is 1/2 Santa Clara and 1/2 Sioux Pot is red with incised feather designs and a pheasant	$185
Kevin Red Starr	1-15/32" x 2-1/2" x 1-1/4"	Sioux Indian living with Santa Clara woman. Black fetish bear, 3 bands of turquoise heishe. Incised arrow feathers, Kiva steps.	$375
Toni Roller	4-9/16" x 4-1/4"	Black, polished, plain with Bear Paw design. Dated 11/91	$250
Camilio Sunflower Tafoya	1-9/16" x 1-5/16"	Buff background, incised antelope dancers, 5 antelope feathers on head dress, blue color on decorations. #985WAO	$850
Ray Tafoya	1-1/2" x 1-1/4"	Red pot incised hummingbird, leaves, blue and yellow - Trademark: Mountains	$300
Ramon Tapia	3/4" x 2-1/4" x 1-13/16"	Turtle, black on black	$35

SANTO DOMINGO PUEBLO

Artist, (alphabetically)	Size	Description	Cost
Manuelita Lovato	5-15/16" x 4-3/8"	Jar is polished, mahogany color, incised mimbres lizard, turquoise stone eyes, lizard outlined with coral. Stopper is brass inlaid with turquoise mother of pearl, jet, spiny oyster shell and sugalite	$1600

ZIA PUEBLO

Artist, (alphabetically)	Size	Description	Cost
Elizabeth Medina	12-11/16" x 2-3/4"	Split tail bird, floral designs	$50
Eusebia Shije	6-15/16" x 5-1/2"	Pot, buff background, split tail wide eyed bird, Kiva steps, corn. Some micaous clay in designs.	$175

ZUNI PUEBLO

Artist, (alphabetically)	Size	Description	Cost
Quanita Kalestewa	8-3/16" x 9"	White and black owl, spread wings, 2 owlets on wings	$500
Ruddell Lanjose	2-1/16" x 2-7/8"	Owl, black and white, yellow beak	$25
Priscilla Peynesta	1-1/8" x 2-5/8"	Saucer shape, brown geometric designs outside, applicated lizard, cattails and tadpoles inside	$45

INDEX